Maybe I Don't Belong Here

DAVID HAREWOOD

Maybe I Don't Belong Here

A Memoir of Race, Identity,
Breakdown and Recovery

Foreword by David Olusoga

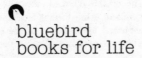

bluebird
books for life

First published 2021 by Bluebird
an imprint of Pan Macmillan
The Smithson, 6 Briset Street, London EC1M 5NR
EU representative: Macmillan Publishers Ireland Ltd, 1st Floor,
The Liffey Trust Centre, 117–126 Sheriff Street Upper,
Dublin 1, D01 YC43
Associated companies throughout the world
www.panmacmillan.com

ISBN HB 978–1–5290–6413–1
ISBN TPB 978–1–5290–6414–8

Content warning: please note that this book details the author's experience
of mental distress and psychosis resulting in hospitalization. Some readers
may find the nature of the themes discussed challenging.

1 3 5 7 9 8 6 4 2

A CIP catalogue record for this book is available from the British Library.

Typeset in Warnock Pro by Palimpsest Book Production Limited, Falkirk, Stirlingshire
Printed and bound by CPI Group (UK) Ltd, Croydon, CR0 4YY

MIX
Paper from
responsible sources
FSC® C116313

Visit **www.panmacmillan.com** to read more about all our books
and to buy them. You will also find features, author interviews and
news of any author events, and you can sign up for e-newsletters
so that you're always first to hear about our new releases.

Contents

To my father.

I was too young to understand what was happening to you when you were experiencing your struggle with mental illness, you rode out the storm alone. It's only now I've written this book that I realise I never got the chance to sit and talk with you about the times those rough winds ripped through our minds. In that respect, I've realised this all too late. I went away to follow my dreams, life and work taking me to other places, and though I did my best to get to see you whenever I could it was never enough. Thank heavens for Sandra. And when another storm came to ravage your mind, this time blasting away your capacity, came a time when it was just enough to sit with you and see the occasional spark in your eye. You were still Dad.

I was in America when I heard the news, heard the news the storm was over. You'd found peace, finally, a place to rest after your long, hard journey, sheltered away now, protected from the harsh winds. Get some sleep, Dad. Thank you for the car rides, the truck trips and the jacket. Thank you for the train pass and for signing the paperwork I needed to secure my grant to go to RADA. You set me up in so many ways, Dad, I'm not sure if I ever I got the chance tell you. I hope you knew it, they all know it now.

This is for you, Dad. Sleep well.

Foreword

When I first met David Harewood, we spoke incessantly for over an hour. We were attending a television industry party, a plush gathering in which guests are expected to circulate and network; the savviest amongst them seeking out valuable face-time with influential commissioners and channel controllers. What you are not supposed to do at such events is enter into a long and intense conversation with a single person to the exclusion of everything and everyone else.

I wanted to talk to David Harewood not because he is a Hollywood actor or the star of TV dramas; the room was full of other famous people. I wanted to talk to him about a season of TV programmes that we had both, separately, appeared in, the previous year. My part in that season had been a documentary in which I had returned to the street in which I had lived as a teenager, back in the 1980s. That street is the site of the home where my inter-racial family had been forced out after a relentless campaign of attacks launched by the thugs of the National Front. This confrontation with my own past had been important and necessary. By being open about my own experiences I was able to demonstrate to viewers how deep the wounds left by racism can run, lingering on decades after the events in question. It had made the documentary more impactful.

Yet despite my professional rationalisation of my decision, when the series was broadcast I felt extraordinarily exposed and uncomfortable. A painful experience I had rarely discussed even with my mother and siblings suddenly became public knowledge. I was asked to speak about it in radio interviews and comment about it in newspapers. Talking about racism publicly, not in the abstract but in raw and personal terms, made me feel that I had broken some unwritten, self-imposed rule. Not long after the series was broadcast, in the midst of my discomfort, I watched another documentary that was part of the same season. Within that programme, to my intense relief, David Harewood gave an interview in which he too spoke candidly of his encounters with British racism. As David recounted shocking experiences from his past, describing them in stark detail, suddenly I felt less alone and less exposed. David's decision to talk openly about what had happened to him seemed somehow to validate my own. I later discovered, from the letters and emails sent by viewers who had watched that season of programmes, that other people of colour had been deeply affected by watching well-known (and in David Harewood's case A-list famous) Black people discussing racism and its impact upon their lives in such frank and personal terms.

Meeting David Harewood a year later at that party gave me an opportunity to explain what his openness had meant to me, how it had reassured me that my own decision to discuss my past had been the right one. We talked about why it was we had never previously felt able to discuss such experiences publicly, and of how so many other Black people had similar stories to tell; stories that only seemed to emerge occasionally and always in private settings. Like many Black people who had encountered the racism of Britain in the 1970s and 1980s, David and I had locked away not just our memories of racist incidents but also, and perhaps more importantly, our memories of how these events had been damaging assaults on our sense of self.

In this book David Harewood writes with rare honesty and fearless self-analysis about exactly such experiences; his upbringing and his encounters with racism from childhood onwards. He explores how the hostility of strangers collided with his developing sense of self and his relationship to Britain and with his own Blackness. Such experiences, combined with other factors, ultimately led to what David describes as the 'deepest darkest moment' in his life; his descent into psychosis at the age of 23.

With equal candour David plots the story of his recovery; a long journey that took him from Birmingham's Hollymoor Psychiatric Hospital to the lights of Hollywood. This book is, in itself, a physical manifestation of that hopeful journey, the process of writing these pages demanding the painful disinterring of long-buried details from David's darkest of moments and a confrontation with the contents of a file containing the medical records from his weeks in Hollymoor Hospital.

The reticence felt by many Black Britons when it comes to talking frankly about their experiences of racism and racial violence is very often accompanied by an even deeper resistance to discussing the issue of mental health. Yet the need for such discussions are arguably greater and more urgent amongst Black Britons than any other demographic. Within Britain's Black communities there exists a mental health crisis, the details of which are largely debated through statistics. Those numbers reveal, amongst other things, that Black people in Britain are far more likely than white people to suffer forms of mental ill-health that lead to them being hospitalised. However, no matter how shocking such statistics might be, and no matter how skilfully and sensitively they are deployed by journalists and the authors of reports, they remain just statistics, mere numbers that are incapable of conveying the human toll of this crisis. By bravely recounting his own experiences, of both his psychosis and his recovery, David makes real and tangible a phenomenon that too often is met with hushed silence and inaction.

Some readers might be surprised that a memoir written by such a celebrated actor explores the politics of race and diversity as much as the craft of the stage. Yet in our society when a Black person writes or speaks about race and racism their words are always regarded as political. Even today, after the murder of George Floyd and the great wave of protest, learning and acknowledgement that followed, there are still people who – with no sense of embarrassment – confidently assert that they just 'don't see race,' encouraging others to affect a similar myopia. To entertain that particular delusion and to imagine oneself capable of that specific impossibility is also to proclaim enormous privilege.

When Black people attempt to travel through life unaware of their race, as David Harewood's story intimately reveals, they place themselves in acute danger. Although Black people, like all people, forge identities that are multi-layered and complex, built on the foundations of family, nationality or class, and shaped by loyalties to a region, a football team or a profession, such identities remain externally invisible. 'I was Black and I had completely underestimated the significance of that reality' writes David on the pages that follow.

Repeated encounters with racism over a lifetime can, and in David Harewood's case undoubtedly did, broaden and deepen the

gulf that inevitably exists between internal and external percep-
tions, between the two sides of what W.E.B. Du Bois described as
the Double Consciousness that Black people are forced to inhabit
while navigating within a racialised society. In a police file the
young David, full of potential and promise, but in need of help in
the midst of a psychotic episode, is reduced to 'a large Black man,'
a stereotype that diminishes a person to their physicality, a Black
body to be feared. Books that address these issues, particularly in
the British context, are rare. Books that do so with such naked
honesty rarer still.

David Olusoga, 2021.

A Letter to the Reader

First of all, I have to be honest, this is not what you might call a straight-up autobiography. If you're looking for tales of the high life, of the glam and the glitter, this book probably isn't for you. The shops are full of fluffy celebrity exposés charting the drama of fame and fortune, and if that's what you're expecting, you might want to ask for your money back.

That's not to say I won't be using this book to tell my story, the tale of a Black kid from Small Heath in Birmingham who dared to dream of a life amongst Hollywood stars; a kid who ended up at dinner one night with Al Pacino and shaking the hand of my all-time favourite, Sidney Poitier, at a Hollywood awards ceremony. I'd be foolish not to include those kinds of memories. But I'm writing this book not to look back at *what* happened to me over my fifty-five years, but as an attempt to understand *why* it happened. I want to examine the impact of my personal history on my mental health and my life. Despite having been sectioned twice, I have been able to build a successful career. In sharing my story, I hope I can offer some hope to those who continue to struggle with their mental health or who feel shame about past episodes of mental illness.

Thirty years ago, fresh out of drama school, I had what I now understand to be a psychotic breakdown. I spent weeks walking all over London, sometimes throughout the night, talking to complete strangers and following them wherever they led me. I'd black out only to regain consciousness in a completely different part of town, hours later, afraid and with absolutely no idea what had happened in the interval. Had it not been for some extraordinary friends who decided amongst themselves that I needed to be hospitalised, I might have vanished into the London night for good. Worse still, I could have taken heed of the incredibly real and convincing voices in my head and simply thrown myself off Westminster Bridge. Instead, I found myself sectioned under the Mental Health Act and kept on a locked ward. Nobody was willing or able to offer any explanation for what I was experiencing.

When I look back, it's clear that I came close to death. Many men, Black men in particular, have died being restrained by the police whilst experiencing psychotic symptoms. I'm absolutely convinced that had I been in America at the time of my breakdown, I'd most likely be dead. I'm acutely aware of just how much I struggled against those trying to subdue me when I was sectioned. It took not one or two but six police officers to hold me down. One false move by me or any of them could have ended my life.

Although I was hospitalised twice in quick succession, I only recovered my sanity at home with my caring, nurturing mother. After those terrifying episodes, I managed to continue my career as an actor remarkably quickly, becoming the first Black actor to be cast as Othello at the Royal National Theatre, as well as appearing in a string of acclaimed international theatre productions. I also played a critical role in the Emmy and Golden Globe-winning

American drama series *Homeland* and bagged a Spirit Award nomination for Best Actor. I guess you could say it has been quite the turnaround!

I've never made a secret of my former mental health troubles. In fact, the story of my breakdown has been a late-night tale told to drunken friends. But I had no idea of the significance of my journey into madness until a couple of years ago when I decided to examine the facts in the award-winning BBC documentary *Psychosis and Me*. During filming I discovered the extent of my breakdown and began to understand its roots. I was confronted with the unbearable pain and confusion from that time in my life, when I was just twenty-three years of age. A pain buried so deep in my subconscious that its existence was a barely remembered dream.

Delving into the causes of my breakdown has involved reconnecting with my struggle to forge a sense of identity and belonging as a Black British man, and the many conflicts I had experienced around race, nationality and acceptance all came flooding back and took me right to the moment my uncertainty began: my first direct experience of racist abuse. That single encounter shattered my perception of myself, splitting my identity in two.

A small crack appeared, perhaps just the faintest fissure at first, but over the years it grew wider and wider. Caught between the two halves of my identity, I disappeared into the space between and woke up in a mental institution. I had completely lost my mind.

The public reaction to *Psychosis and Me* took me completely by surprise. All sorts of different people approached me in the street to recount their own experiences of psychosis. I realised that rather than being isolated in my experience, countless people had sons, daughters, mothers and fathers who had lived through something similar themselves. They were thankful that I had spoken out. I began to recognise that what had happened to me was very common, but rarely talked about. There didn't seem to be a language in which people could easily discuss the topic. MIND, the mental health charity, informed me that the night the film aired, calls about psychosis rose by 107 per cent. Little did I realise that the documentary was just starting to lift the lid on my own understanding of the past.

The stigma surrounding psychosis is intense and many are either too embarrassed or ashamed to talk about or admit their experience. This reluctance strikes me as odd, because I've always seen my breakdown as a truly remarkable event in my life. It helped unlock my understanding of myself, a process that is ongoing to this day.

It was only after making the documentary and talking about it that I learned the shocking facts about Black mental health in the UK. According to the latest government figures, Black people are four times more likely to be detained under the Mental Health Act than white people and are far more likely to be diagnosed with schizophrenia and psychosis. Out of sixteen specific ethnic groups, Black Caribbean people have the highest rates of detention in psychiatric hospital. Clearly, there is something about living in Britain that is tough for Black people.

I can certainly attest that even on a purely professional level it's been difficult for me as a Black actor. Back when I first started out, there were very few good roles for Black actors on television outside the narrow band of law and order figures, roles which rarely had depth or authority. Whilst on stage I could look forward to tackling complex Shakespearean characters night after night, on television it was another world entirely. Over the years this would frustrate me and, as the parts dwindled, I feared things were pretty much over. Thankfully America came calling just in time. The weekend I jetted off to shoot the pilot episode of *Homeland* I was down to my last eighty quid!

I understand what it's like to be skint, to lack opportunities, to see others getting ahead of you. I've also experienced racism, both overt and subtle, and I've been outspoken about it, too. Britain has deep pockets of racism and that may surprise some, but not me. Without doubt the impact of racism can contribute to the development of psychosis. Denying this basic reality risks pushing people of colour further and further away from mental health services and away from the help they so desperately need. The numbers don't lie.

My own breakdown was a cry for help that I couldn't appreciate at the time. Uncovering its origins while writing this book has been difficult, but what I have discovered has given me an immense freedom. Now it's possible to consider my entire life from a whole new perspective. In moving through post-traumatic stress, I have even discovered some 'post-traumatic growth'. I'm grateful for the opportunity to understand the root of my insecurities and vulnerability and I have written this book as an attempt to help other people connect mental ill-health to something beyond themselves.

I was extremely lucky to survive my brush with psychosis and, although I was sectioned twice in short succession, I have never had any further episodes or needed further medication. That's not true for everyone. There are many Black men, in particular, who continue to be affected by these issues but avoid getting the support they need because of traumatic experiences with mental health services. Other chronic sufferers find themselves trapped in a cycle of hospitalisation, poverty and, often, crime. This can be an impossibly hard pattern to break and when racism is thrown into the mix, the emotional build-up can have explosive and sometimes dangerous consequences.

As a Black British man I believe it is vital that I tell this story. It may be just a single account from one person of colour, but my hope is that it might be enough to change some opinions or, more importantly, stop someone else from spinning completely out of control.

Chapter One

There Ain't No Black in the Union Jack

One of my earliest memories is of when I was three, aimlessly wandering out the back door of our house in Arthur Street, Birmingham. I was looking for Roger, my elder brother. I'd no sooner set foot into the yard than I was struck in the head with a rock as big as a tennis ball. I don't remember feeling any physical pain at the time, but I do remember wailing in shock and calling for my brother, my idol. I was still so young that I couldn't pronounce my 'R's or 'G's so I cried out for 'Woyer, Woyer!' Roger was nowhere to be seen but my loud screams attracted the attention of my mother, who was nearby chopping wood for the fire.

Mayleen Harewood is a proud Bajan woman, hard-working and fiercely protective of her children. She instantly had a good idea of who was responsible for throwing the rock. It wasn't the first time our troublesome white neighbours had caused her concern, and she led me inside, cleaned up the blood streaming from my forehead and told us all not to leave the house. Then she marched off to the local police station. Upon arrival my mother approached the officer on duty behind his desk and said with calm, supressed Bajan rage:

'Excuse me. My youngest child has just been hit in the head with a rock by one of our neighbours. Officer, when I heard my child scream I was chopping wood for a fire. So help me God, if I'd have caught the person responsible for chucking it, I would have buried that chopper in their skull. I ask you to please come round and talk to these people or by Christ, you'll be over later taking them to the morgue and me off to prison!'

She meant every word of it. The policeman took down some details and later that day knocked on our neighbours' door and had a word. Not that it stopped the trouble. A couple of weeks later, early on a Saturday morning, my mother called us all down from our bedrooms for breakfast and we came running in eager anticipation of one of her Saturday specials – a full English: bacon, egg, sausage, beans and toast with all the trimmings, yum! But, just as we got to the table, a brick came crashing through the window, bouncing off the table and landing on the floor in front of us. I'll never forget the sight, my favourite English breakfast, cooked and ready to eat, covered in glass.

'Go back upstairs . . . I'll call you when I've cooked something fresh,' Mum said.

We moved away shortly afterwards and in the spring of 1973 took up residence in Small Heath, a tough working-class neighbourhood that was respectable and tidy. Although I was still quite young, I had the impression we'd moved up in the world. Oldknow Road was lined with identical little houses and tiny front gardens with some families going to the trouble of painting their front walls in an effort to look posh.

There were trees on either side of the road and the street itself had a gentle sloping hill at one end. The other end was bordered by the main road, Coventry Road, with lots of shops and regular buses into town, perfect for a young family of four. We settled in quickly. The house had two rooms downstairs, a kitchen and an indoor bathroom (result!), plus three bedrooms, one for my sister Sandra, one shared between my two older brothers Roger and Paul and me, and the last for Mum and Dad. It was a fine little house where all my childhood memories now gather like old friends.

As far as I was aware, we were the only Black family on our end of the street. There were a couple of Indian and Pakistani families towards the other end of the road, but apart from that, the street was filled with white English and Irish families with names like Davidson, Duggan and Lovegrove. We lived next door to the Davidsons and at first they weren't too pleased about their new dark-skinned neighbours. However, as time passed, they mellowed and actually became rather friendly. But then just as we were hitting our stride in the new house, somebody put an envelope full of shit through our letter box, which is something that to this day still puzzles me. I mean, why go to the trouble of collecting your own shit, carrying it down the street and posting it? It was the very idea of doing it which really disgusted me, not particularly the racial aggravation. Mum and Dad just cleaned up the mess with a bemused shrug and continued on with their day.

I was probably around five now and I had definitely picked up that some people in the area were none too pleased to see Black faces around. I remember being a little afraid to go outside of my house and I had a fear of the world beyond our front garden. It was probably this same fear that caused me to cry my eyes out on my first day of school. I can remember clinging on to my mother's arm as we made the short journey from our house, up the road to St Benedict's Junior School. Upon arrival, I completely refused to let Mum go. The idea of being away from my parents' protective care filled me with terror. Mum had to work hard to get me inside. As it was, I loved my first day at school. In fact, I continued to enjoy school right up until the day I left at eighteen. At school I discovered the joys of friendship and laughter that made me thrive. I flourished being around people and school provided me with an assortment of wonderful experiences and deep connections, some of which I still have today.

In time, I'd make the journey to school and home again on my own, but in the early days I felt safer in the company of my mother. I looked forward to seeing her face at the end of the school day, waiting for me just beyond the school fence. As I grew older it became clear that the streets outside my home could really be dangerous. Mum and Dad began cautiously speaking to us about how there were certain white people who didn't like us. We were told to watch out for one another whenever we left the house. I can remember starting to watch white people when I walked past them in the street. Some would smile and nod as they passed with open, friendly faces, while others carried on without so much as a glance. But every now and again there'd be a look in the eye that chilled me. I couldn't explain it, it was just something I felt in my bones, and every time I saw someone like that, I looked away and quickened my step.

When I was seven years old, matters became irrevocably clear. It was an incident I'll never forget for it created a rupture that lasts until this very day. Playing alone outside my house one day, I noticed an older, white gentleman walking towards me from across the road. He wasn't charging at me so I didn't feel danger, but I could tell it was a purposeful walk. I stopped what I was doing and watched as he got closer. When he was finally within arm's length, his face a picture of hatred and anger, he leaned in towards me and said:

'Get the fuck out of my country, you little Black bastard!'

I was shocked and rooted to the spot. He glared at me for a moment, before slowly turning and walking away. I watched as he strode off, working out what he had just said to me. 'His' country? Was it not mine too? Perhaps it wasn't? I was piecing it together, my imaginary game now over, replaced by more serious thought.

Maybe I don't belong here?

And that's when it happened, the two halves of me split. There was now a Black half and an English half and I could feel myself slowly coming apart. At times in my life I've been able to fuse these two halves together, but occasionally the gap between them is just too big and I struggle. How can I be English when much of England refuses to accept my Blackness and makes it clear that I am not welcome? Sometimes I wonder if it's actually possible to be a Black Englishman. Surely it doesn't make any sense? From that day forward, keeping the two parts of my identity joined together has been a conscious effort. And when the space between them gets too wide, I lose my bearings. When I had my breakdown, there was an absolute firestorm of thoughts and confusion. I felt powerless to stop my fall and the longer it continued, the faster I fell.

These days I'm more watchful and more aware of the space in between the two halves. I'm able to judge the distance now. When they drift apart, I move with them, building mental pathways back towards wholeness. It's a constant battle. Even in my professional life.

He's too English!

He's not Black enough!

The ground beneath me crumbles. It can be a destructive pattern. It's almost as if my identity feels it's under attack, just like it was on the streets of Birmingham all those years earlier.

Britain in the late 1960s and '70s was an environment where Black kids like me were often subject to random and unforeseen racist attacks. Although I felt safe at school and could afford to clown around, enjoying the freedom of a safe space, on the streets and on the way home, it was another matter entirely. Some days would pass without incident, almost as if all was well, then suddenly, out of nowhere, from a passing car I would hear:

'Nigger!'

And my whole body would tense at some random voice calling out in the afternoon sun. Or there would be monkey noises accompanying me as I walked down the street.

'Oi! You little Black bastard. Where you going?'

Keep walking, pay no attention, just keep going, nearly home.

But perhaps the most symbolic example of this rupture within my identity was this catchy little ditty:

'There Ain't No Black in the Union Jack.'

White guys took such joy singing this tune back in the day. Its rumbling menace had the peculiar effect of actually matching the rhythm of my stride as I walked past them.

Repeated again and again, the phrase hung in the air like a football chant and left no doubt as to whom it was directed. I remember leaving my house for school the morning of the Queen's Silver Jubilee in 1975 and seeing the whole street decked out in little Union Jack flags. It was the first time I'd seen so many and as I walked along I began to notice something. I saw that there was indeed *no* black in the Union Jack – the menacing chant was correct. I had a growing sense of fear as a child that the Union Jack flag was a physical symbol of my 'otherness' and once again my identity took a hit.

How can I be a Black Englishman?

As the '70s progressed, the Union Jack flag became the proud symbol of people the Black community feared most on the streets, namely skinheads and the National Front. These people would, in no uncertain terms, attack Black kids like me on sight. The National Front, a right-wing, anti-immigration movement, had rapidly gained popularity across large areas of the country, especially in industrial, working-class cities like Birmingham. With its car and machinery plants looking to boost capacity and in need of labourers, the rise of the National Front was an immediate threat. The NF stood in opposition to the growing numbers of Black and brown workers arriving from abroad looking for jobs. Now, no matter how old you were, you had to be watchful. Attacks could be brutal. Many of these guys even wore Union Jacks prominently on their bomber jackets, and one particular skinhead I remember had a Union Jack tattooed on his face.

If you were Black, you became adept at sensing these attacks, almost as if you had a superpower or Spidey-sense!

A rapidly slowing car . . .

The sound of multiple doors opening . . .

One signal was all we needed. A quick glance over the shoulder to see how many men and what they were carrying – iron bars, chains or knives – and we were gone! Up and over a six-foot fence like it was a footstool, down an entryway, over a wall, under impossible spaces and we were well on our way, hardly ever caught. Hiding was never an option as occasionally elderly neighbours, sick of us being in their rose gardens retrieving our footballs, would lean out of upstairs windows and direct our pursuers to our whereabouts:

'He went behind that car!'

'I think there's one of them ran through Nelly's garden! Check behind the shed.'

No. Best to keep going, best to keep running until you're sure you're out of sight and safe, which was when all the Union Jacks had disappeared. Until next time.

To this day I've never been able to get over that feeling and whenever I see the flag I still instinctively stiffen. There's much about the country that I love, its strength of character, culture and passion, and I have felt pride in the achievements of my fellow citizens. But this is old memory, deep and seared into my psyche. I know the fear is not completely rational. After all, there are many who fly the flag with pride today and mean me no harm at all. Yet for years the Union Jack meant danger and I had to be careful of those who sported it.

The seventy-fifth anniversary of VE Day fell in 2020 and again the flags were out in number, just as they were during the Brexit debates. I still find myself on guard, on my toes. During the Black Lives Matter counter-demonstrations in central London in the summer of the same year, it was no surprise to me at all to see the far right marching alongside the Union Jack, waving it and singing 'God Save The Queen'. They looked like the guys who used to chase me all those years ago.

Racism is part of the fabric of my life in the UK. It's as familiar to me as the start of the football season or the theme tune of *News at Ten*. I've grown up with it. I know what it looks like. So you can imagine my astonishment when the government produced a race report in 2021, the Sewell report, that totally diminished my lived experience and told me that the things I knew to be true were just a myth. This dismissal of my experience erodes trust. I sometimes watch young Black British athletes at the Olympics drape themselves in the Union Jack when they win and I'm genuinely envious. As a direct result of my experiences I would struggle to embrace the flag like that. To me, it is a symbol of a near constant struggle to keep the two halves of myself from coming apart.

Chapter Two

Just Like That

Romeo Cornelius Harewood left Barbados late in the summer of 1957 and arrived in England six weeks later, ready to begin a brand-new life of adventure in the country's second city, Birmingham. He'd taken a big step, a leap of faith, and landed in the Mother Country ready to roll up his sleeves and get to work. He set right to it.

An industrious man, my father was good with his hands and more than ready to work long hours to make a living. Birmingham held opportunity and promise and 'Joe', as my father was known for short, was willing to get the job done, but I remember him telling me it was tough to find work at first. He would never be drawn on why getting a job had been so difficult:

'There were a couple of stupid people, you know. You just tell them to bugger off!'

Before too long, he landed a position working for British Rail. He wasn't actually a train driver – although when I was young I remember thinking he was! Instead, he drove enormous lorries and trailers around for 'Freightliner', a company that distributed cargo carried by the rail network, travelling across the country from day to day. It was a solid blue-collar job with lots of benefits. He made an effort to look the part, taking pride in his uniform and checking his blazer was in place over his shirt, tie and jumper. My father was all in blues and greys topped off by a little black cap! I asked him to get me one of those jackets in the '80s when I was about fourteen. I repeatedly asked him and he finally gave in and got me one. When he handed it to me, he looked puzzled. I'm not sure he quite understood why I'd want it, but I was really happy he'd delivered. I thought it looked so cool! I used to wear it hanging around with the sleeves rolled up *Miami Vice* style!

My father's work clothes weren't the only perk of his job. One of the benefits was free rail travel for dependents, 'subject to inspection', of course! When I decided to pursue acting at sixteen, he got me a handy 'authorisation card' that I used to get to all my London auditions, including the one for RADA. I guess I owe a lot to my father's ability to get himself a good job, maybe even more than I realised.

Joe married my mother, Mayleen, in 1963 and the two of them quickly began the search for a place raise a family. We stayed in a couple of places, temporary housing in different parts of the city, before settling in a lovely little house in the Small Heath area of Birmingham and that's where this story really begins. I remember my dad's nice car and the way he took pride in how it looked. He'd take us on long drives to the beach, either to Blackpool or Rhyl or Weston-super-Mare. We spent hours in that car, just the family on a day out. At the beach, we'd play in the sand for a couple of hours, eat our sandwiches and head home for some telly. I enjoyed being on the road with my dad. I loved all the movement and the things racing by the window. I particularly liked it when he took me out in his big truck! Sitting up in the passenger seat, looking out across the country as it raced by, vast green fields that seemed to go on for an eternity, and then we would make our way to huge container depots filled with giant cranes where the trucks would unload their goods. You had to be pretty accurate backing an articulated truck into some of those tight spaces. I was impressed by my father's ability to manoeuvre that thing. Once the truck was in place, haulers unloaded the goods. It was generally a thirty- to forty-minute job unloading the trailer but my father was adamant he would wait no longer than twenty-five minutes, and as soon as physically possible we'd be back out on the road.

I loved being up high in the cabin, looking down on all the passing cars as the hours rolled by. I was quite shy as a young kid and my father was pretty quiet himself, but from time to time he'd ask me if I was okay because I'd hardly said a word.

'I'm okay.'

And he'd nod. I'd drift straight back into my own private fantasies, staring out of the window daydreaming of fighter jets swooping down on my side of the truck as we raced along the motorway at speed. The pilots were carrying out a top secret mission to intercept my father. He had a dangerous load in the trailer, it was becoming unstable. I may need to jettison! More than likely I'd seen some plot on the television that had caught my imagination, in James Bond or *Thunderbirds*, and it had stuck with me.

Although he drove many miles in a single day, Dad always preferred to sleep at home and not in the truck. He would park it up on the street outside the house. That way he could get up early and continue his journey in the morning. He did this for years until one of our neighbours complained to the council.

'He's parking his bleedin' lorry on the pavement again. Nelly! Phone the council! He's cracked all the new paving stones.'

He hadn't. But it was a huge truck so he was told he couldn't park it there anymore.

He was always up so early my dad, way before I'd get up for school. I remember the sound of his keys jingling in his pockets as he walked past my bedroom in the morning headed down to get ready for work. It cut through my dreams as I slept and reminded me of his presence. It was comforting.

My dad worked hard, but it was my mother who hardly ever sat herself down. If she wasn't cooking, cleaning, washing or ironing, she'd be carrying bags of shopping from the Woolworth's up the road or generally making sure the house was together. She was sharp, young, strong and dependable – a good catch. She had a little fire in her, too, which is probably why Joe decided to put some rules down as the years ticked by:

'Monday to Friday I work for you. But the weekends are all mine.'

He'd work hard for the family during the week but Friday night to Monday morning was 'Joe Time' down the pub with his mates or playing cricket with his West Indian friends on a Sunday. Sometimes we'd go and watch him play. He was well turned out in his cricket whites and often his friends came back to the house for drinks or food. Black people weren't allowed into some of the bars and clubs so someone would hire a school hall and they'd meet up for dances and get-togethers, where those who had settled from the Caribbean would drink rum, listen to music, cook up food and talk of old times and new. He was happy: he had a good job, a family and a nice place to live. His leap of faith seemed to have paid off and he made himself a little castle where he was King of the Land of Harewood.

I loved growing up in that house. Some of my happiest memories are there, sitting alongside my family in front of the telly, watching the shows. That was where I first fell in love with the idea of performing. Having the power to hold an audience's attention the way entertainers did was mesmerising to me. How was that possible? I was fascinated.

I was about eight or nine years old by this point, walking home on my own a little more comfortably, and my routine was set.

Jingle jingle.

(That was my father . . .)

Up for school.

Breakfast and telly.

Quick splash and dash in the bathroom and then I'd wait in the front room watching out the porch window for a bus to come down the hill. I'd make a run for it as soon as I saw it. It was always tight, depending on how fast the bus was moving. Luckily, I was quick, and usually made it, although there were some drivers who drove faster when they saw a Black boy running and drove off after only stopping a short while. They drove off on purpose. Just another one of those things you get used to. No biggie. I'll just be a tiny bit late.

Dad would usually be in his favourite chair when I got home from school, still in his driver's uniform, sitting square in front of the TV with a can of beer perched on the arm of the chair. If he wasn't going out, he'd be there all night and hardly move at all, occasionally instructing one of us kids to get up and change the channel when he wanted to check out what was on the other side. I usually volunteered for that job. I was always keen to see what else was on. Sometimes Dad would fall asleep in his chair and would be snoring quite loudly. Then I'd creep up and try to change the channel without him noticing, but he'd wake up as soon as he heard the noise of the channel changing and say:

'I was watching that.'

And I'd have to change it back to *World in Action* for another hour of far-flung strife.

We watched all sorts of things. As soon as Mum had cooked and we'd all stuffed our faces, it was telly time. A Harewood household tradition. Get the telly on and settle down for a fabulous night of British entertainment! And there was nothing I enjoyed more. If there's one thing that inspired me to be an actor, it was those nights in front of the television, especially all the scripted shows and the live audience stuff. The characters leaped off the screen for me in ways I couldn't quite understand. They sparked my imagination.

I remember being glued to the TV whenever I was home. I loved the movies and the comedies and the dramas. Even though I didn't know it, I was falling in love with everything about it. When Mum and Dad watched British sitcoms, the house was filled with raucous laughter. Both of my parents had the most incredibly animated laughs. Extraordinary physical convulsions, howls of deep, whole laughter.

'BWAHAHAAAAAA HA HA HA HA!

HAAAAAAA HAA HAA HAA HAA!'

They would bend themselves double as they ran out of air, only to take a short, sharp breath and let out the second wave of the laugh, which would throw them back in the opposite direction. It was funnier watching them laugh than it was watching the television! Our next-door neighbour once told my mother they knew if anything good was on the telly by hearing our laughter through the walls. If I could take a snapshot of those days, I'd say they were some of the happiest in my life. The room, lit only by the screen and the orange glow from the electric fire, and my family huddled together to take in the evening's entertainment.

My father usually had his evening all planned out and would flick between the three channels to catch his favourite shows: *Rising Damp, Opportunity Knocks, The Professionals, The Sweeney, It Ain't Half Hot Mum, Some Mothers do 'Ave 'Em, The Two Ronnies, Crossroads* and *Coronation Street, George and Mildred,*

The Sky at Night, Citizen Smith, Terry and June – some of the best scripted comedy of the day. He couldn't get enough of any of them. My favourite was always Tommy Cooper, a man so funny he would make my belly hurt. To explain his act can't quite do it justice, but basically he was a bad magician whose tricks often failed, but he was so funny at presenting them that you didn't care. He was a giant of a man, well over six feet tall, and he wore a red fez for some reason, the kind you'd find in a Moroccan souk. It always looked perfect sitting atop his huge head. He'd tell jokes and funny stories as he made his way through the various tricks and he had the audience in the palm of his hand.

'I went to the doctor the other day. I said, "Doctor, it hurts when I do that." (Waving his arm.) He said, "Don't do it then!"'

Gags that were simple, uncomplicated and so funny. Tommy Cooper must have made a huge impression on me because just before I was sectioned in the Whittington Psychiatric Hospital, I turned up to a psych evaluation wearing a red fez. I wasn't thinking too clearly, because I'd written on it with a dark felt-tip pen and stuck a yellow Monopoly deed in a hole I'd sliced in the top of the hat. I'm not sure why I did that but it obviously meant something to me. I'd had the hat for years but it seems it spoke to me that morning and I channelled Tommy Cooper whilst I slipped into a psychotic breakdown.

Tommy Cooper's talent for physical comedy was off the scale and his command of the audience was so complete that you could forgive his rubbish magic. Sometimes his tricks were so terrible, he'd completely abandon them halfway through. Eventually he'd get it together and, with a simple sleight of hand when the trick was done, he'd look to the watching millions and say:

'Just Like That!'

And his big hands would dangle out in front of him!

Just like that indeed.

Just like that we were soaking in British culture. Assimilating and ironing out any other traces of our identity. We were becoming British, whatever that meant. I began to associate with all these characters drifting into my consciousness every night and I would even try to mimic them. Leonard Rossiter, Eric Sykes and Frankie Howerd. I watched how they moved and brought an audience to attention and then had the crowd hanging on every word. When famous actors turned up on talk shows discussing their work, I sat engrossed. Jack Lemmon on *Parkinson* and Tony Curtis on *Wogan*. I marvelled at it all. A little Black boy loving Kirk Douglas and Spencer Tracy, the Westerns and the cowboy flicks too. I consumed British content every single day and some of it the best British television of the age – Morecambe and Wise, Benny Hill, *Are You Being Served?*, Monty Python, Spike Milligan, Les Dawson, Dick Emery, Dave Allen – all of them so enjoyable to watch.

There were hardly ever any Black people on British TV when I was growing up. It was *so* rare that one time I was playing football with my two brothers in the playground at the back of our house, when my sister came tearing out of the kitchen, ran to the bottom of the garden and screamed through the fence:

'Roger! Paul! David! There's a Black man on the telly!'

Instantly the three of us turned and ran for the house. We leaped up the wall at the bottom of our garden that separated our house from the playground, pulled back the wire fence and slipped through and into our garden and carried on running.

Gotta be quick!

You know the Black character's not going to make it to the end of the movie so you HAVE TO RUN IF YOU WANT TO CATCH HIS PERFORMANCE!

We flew into the living room and landed in a crumpled heap at my father's feet leering at the screen to see if it was really true. And there he was! It would usually be the fabulous American ex-football star Woody Strode, such a wonderful actor. He'd turn up in so many of those old pictures. Woody Strode played Draba the Black gladiator in *Spartacus* and he was always such an incredible presence. He rarely had any lines but his magnificence didn't need any. He dominated the screen whenever he was on, but unfortunately he always died a 'noble' death in the service of the movie's white hero before the end of the film. If you remember *Spartacus*, he's the character forced to fight Kirk Douglas to the death despite the fact that he kicks Spartacus's arse. Draba inexplicably decides to save Spartacus and launch a kamikaze attack on all the Roman tribunes. Not surprisingly, he's dead within seconds and the movie continues without him. I guess you could say that he had the foresight to know Spartacus was 'the dude' and one of them had to die a noble death. This was the usual arc of Black characters back in the day. They'd volunteer to save the movie's white hero from certain death by fighting the Cyclops or sword-fighting skeletons.

We never understood why the Black characters always made such decisions but we knew it meant they wouldn't last long. Once they'd died we'd usually return to whatever it was we had been doing before. The only other Black faces I saw on the telly back then belonged to the great West Indian cricket team that came over in the summer of 1976 and 'white-washed' a dazzled England team in a blaze of fast balls and shining Black skin! What a summer that was! I'd come home from school and Dad would be in his chair grinning and laughing, cheering every shot as it flashed towards the boundary.

'What's the score, Dad?'

'Greenidge is still batting, son! They can't get him out! HA HAAAAHH!'

The third test. England versus the West Indies. Gordon Greenidge batting in the sun at the Oval and my father cheering every shot! It was a Caribbean summer that year, hot as hell, and the calypso drums played loud and the Oval crowd jumped and cheered as yet another ball flashed towards the boundary.

'And that's through the gap. Don't go running for that!'

Greenidge was masterfully stroking the English bowling all over the pitch! That's probably the happiest I ever saw my father, watching that test match and seeing Black sportsmen dominate the English. I couldn't see it at the time and neither could my father but our 'Black selves', our core Black identity, felt acknowledged that day even though it was only a cricket match. Watching those cricketers made us feel good. We rarely saw Black excellence and these guys were so cool. It made us feel part of something, like we belonged. We were at one with those in the crowd, dancing, drumming, whooping and cheering. We all understood what it was to be Black that day, unapologetically Black. Not 'other' or English. It was a specific identity and it felt good to be on the winning side.

I never spoke to my father about the anxieties I faced on the street. I don't remember ever asking him how to deal with racism, or what I should do to combat the feelings it stirred in me. I sometimes tried to ask him about his early days in the country, almost hoping he'd mention his own encounters with racism so we could discuss it, but he would never talk about it. He'd just shrug it off and change the subject. Not surprising really.

When the Black Lives Matter movement exploded across the globe during the pandemic, I was inundated with requests from various media outlets asking me to 'Come on the show and talk about it.' I turned most of them down and only agreed when I knew and trusted the journalists personally. All too often those interviews can traumatise you all over again, bringing up memories and emotions that are difficult to contain. And, if the interviewer isn't empathetic, you can find yourself the victim of an 'emotional mugging'. Out of nowhere you're fighting difficult emotions and unable to speak. I didn't want to be that guy, and I guess my father didn't want to be that guy either. We had both consumed so much British culture by that point that our English identities had taken over. Seeing white people on the television every single night was the absolute norm, as well as white people in adverts, on cooking shows, comedy shows, game shows, movies, dramas. It all seemed totally normal. Images of beauty were white, the hero was white – everything was white – we were very much living in a 'white space'.

I was so busy assimilating, finding my place in the world and lapping up all things English, I would even turn my nose up at my mother's West Indian food. Can you imagine? My mother's West Indian food in favour of sausage and chips! Unthinkable now. Looking back on it, I was absorbing whiteness without truly understanding what it was doing to me and how it was subtly altering my image of self. With no other way of understanding where I belonged, I focused on what made me feel good – laughing and playing, just like on the TV – and the deeper, more complicated stuff could wait. My mother noticed this and I remember her sometimes talking to me about Blackness and how important it was to hold on to your Black identity, but I wasn't really listening. I understood what she was saying but I pushed back, telling her that I felt I had a handle on how I viewed things. I'd heard the words of Martin Luther King's great 'I Have a Dream' speech and although I didn't quite understand everything he was referencing, it really moved me and imprinted itself on my mind. I remembered him saying he had a dream that his four little children would 'one day live in a nation where they will not be judged by the colour of their skin but by the content of their character'. I felt the power of his words through the TV screen. I felt it in my stomach and I knew it was important.

'One day, right there in Alabama, little Black boys and Black girls will be able to join hands with little white boys and white girls as sisters and brothers.'

But in my mind that was already my reality. I was surrounded by 'little Black boys and Black girls joining hands with little white boys and white girls'; I felt I was already living Dr King's dream. No wonder at the sharp end of my psychotic breakdown it was Martin Luther King's voice that I heard in my head. He'd been with me a long time, guiding me, shaping my world and giving me a vision of what was possible.

One of the few programmes that attempted to depict the prejudice encountered by the average Black Briton was *Till Death Us Do Part*, a sitcom set in London's East End featuring a character called Alf Garnet. Alf was a working-class hero who railed against immigrants and the erosion of Englishness, often referring to Black characters as 'Coons' and 'Wogs'. I'm guessing the show was meant to be challenging, but audiences, surprisingly, loved Alf and forgave his racist attitudes. They saw him as a salt of the earth guy who simply 'told it like it is'. In reality, Alf was saying what most English people really thought and, although it was meant to be a comedy, it had a sharp edge that never really sat comfortably with me. It was sometimes on Dad's watch list but to my young ears Alf's offensive language sounded all too familiar. I'd heard it outside the house, on my way home from school and the guys calling me 'Coon' weren't looking for laughs. Watching that show was actually quite frightening, and I'd leave the room whenever it was on, or tune out and read a comic, the page lit by an orange glow, tilted perfectly for reading by the cat as it stretched out napping in front of the fire.

The Black and White Minstrel Show, a staple of Saturday night viewing, also confused me. My mother and father seemed to watch it with benign amusement, but I hated it. I couldn't understand why it was on. The performers clearly weren't really Black! I didn't understand what they were doing and it made me deeply uncomfortable.

My 'Black self' was still searching to be understood, having been split off from the rest of me by that man's scarring racist remark. The only way I really understood Black culture was through music and there I could identify with the ideas of oppression and love. There was always something cultural and deep I could feel with Black music. But when the music stopped it was back to the everyday. Growing up in a white-centric culture, a 'white space', my Black self hadn't yet fully emerged.

When I look back, it seems astonishing to me that I ever thought a career in acting would work because nearly everybody I saw on television did not look like me. Yet still I thought it might be possible. Maybe I believed in the transformative power of acting, because TV comedians could just put on a silly hat and add a northern accent and they'd suddenly be different characters. That same comedian would play countless characters over the course of an hour-long show and the audience never questioned it. Surely that's how things would be for me, right? If I ever wanted to act? I could be whoever I wanted to be, right?

Truth is, I would pay heavily for being this naive when I finally became an actor. I found that having Black skin significantly reduced the kinds of roles people could 'believe' me in and put a focus on me that was unexpected and difficult to navigate. Eventually my psyche zeroed in on these blocks to my career and the resulting insecurities, all of which contributed to my break-down. I simply hadn't thought about these issues when I dreamed of being a performer and it was quite a shock to my system when my race became the immediate and often central issue. I had started to see the 'white space' as normal, even to the point of feeling as though I belonged in it. In truth, the picture was far more complex. Just like the Tommy Cooper magic act, I had been sucked into an illusion.

It baffles me, looking back to my childhood, that the first foot-ball team I ever supported was Leeds United. They even played in all white! But I didn't see the problem. I simply watched them every week on *Match of the Day* and always looked out for their results. In my mind I was a Leeds United fan and nothing could shake my undying love for Lorimer, Bremner and the magnificent boys in white. One season, I noticed that Leeds were playing Birmingham and I resolved to go and support my team and cheer them on as I had always wanted to do. Back in those days at St Andrew's, the home ground of Birmingham City, the stewards would open the gates at half-time, making it possible to walk in and view the second half of the game for free. I took advantage and decided to walk into the Leeds United half to sit amongst the fans. Huge mistake. I remember walking along the side of the pitch at the away end in order to take a seat, when I started to hear monkey noises coming from Leeds fans to my left. It was only a few at first and I thought it was manageable so I continued walking towards the seats, but soon the monkey noises grew louder until it seemed like ten thousand people were joining in.

'Coon. Nigger. Where the fuck do you think you're going?'

I kept walking for some reason. Perhaps I heard the voice of my mother telling me to 'Hold my head up' as she used to back then. 'Be strong,' she'd say. But it got too much and finally I turned on my heels and began walking back out of the ground in the opposite direction. That was a tough lesson I'll never forget and I haven't been to a football match on my own since. I remember a ground official, a big white guy, calling out to me as I left:

'You okay, son?'

I murmured something and walked away.

My 'English self' believed it would be fine to go and sit amongst a group of Leeds United fans that day. I identified with them so why should I not take my seat?

My 'Black self' absolutely knew it was a bad idea. But I'd hardly got to know that part of myself, so he didn't speak up and warn me.

Chapter Three

The Play's the Thing

I'd always enjoyed playing as a young kid. As early as I can remember, all of us siblings – my brothers Roger and Paul, my sister Sandra and I – were always up to something. On the nights when my father was down the pub and my mother was out for a round of bingo, the house would become our playground. The four of us would get up to all sorts, like jumping into cardboard boxes and hurling ourselves down the stairs. Or, a particular favourite was everyone grabbing a piece of rolled-up newspaper, turning all the lights out and bashing the crap out of whoever you could get your hands on in the dark. Every now and again during the carnage one of us would knock one of my mother's prized ornaments off the shelf and the sound of it smashing would bring our play to an abrupt end. The lights would go on and we'd all stand staring at the broken ornament in horror, wondering how best to glue it back together or whether to just dispose of it completely, praying Mum wouldn't notice. Mostly we'd bin it and hope for the best but Mum was sharper than we gave her credit for and after the second and third of her prized ornaments mysteriously disappeared from her collection, she came out with one of her classics as she left for a night of bingo. As she opened the door, she turned to us with a cold, serious stare and said:

'If I come back and anything break? I goin' tek a piece and CUT U ASS!'

We got the message.

Like many West Indian households at the time we had a front room in our house that was specifically for guests, with the furniture often covered for special occasions and everything kept in immaculate condition, all off limits to us kids. When Mum and Dad's West Indian friends came round, they were treated to the best plates and cutlery and hosted in the front room whilst we milled around and kept ourselves out of the way. They were always very smartly dressed, these West Indian guests, as if they came from another time. They held themselves differently and spoke in beautiful accents, soft and lilting. I could have listened to them all night.

When Mum and Dad were out, however, we'd spend more and more time in this off-limits room, creeping in to investigate the space, scanning my parents' record collection and playing some of their tunes on the big stereo that would occasionally double as a table-tennis table. Lift the lid. Vinyl in the middle, radio and cassette player to the right, turntable to the left. Later, as I grew up, I would spend hours in this room.

Mum and Dad had quite a lot of records back then. The Ink Spots, The Platters, The Stylistics, Bob Marley . . . They even had some Beatles. I used to love looking at the artwork on the sleeves featuring Black guys in sharp suits and lots of flamboyant outfits. To my eternal shame, I confess to sometimes taking some of the records out of their sleeves and skimming them like frisbees over the playground out the back! Dreadful. Classic vinyl flying through the air and smashing into pieces as it hit the concrete surface. My parents lost a lot of good music that way. I think we got told off for it eventually.

On these nights with the four of us playing, I began to express myself a little more and I had a habit of going the extra mile to get a laugh. Sometimes that meant wearing some of my parents' clothes and stomping about the house or even walking up and down the street outside and waving to the people on the buses as they passed by – anything to get a smile from my siblings. One evening when my mum was home, I decided to put my newfound confidence to the test and play a trick on her. Whilst she was in the kitchen, I crept upstairs and grabbed one of her fake fur coats from the wardrobe, slipped into a pair of her high heels, put on one of her prized wigs and snuck out the front door. Meanwhile my sister Sandra, who was in on the gag, told my mother that someone was at the door to see her. When she opened the door, she was caught short for a brief moment wondering who it was before I spun round and surprised her. She burst out laughing when she realised it was me and I was *so* happy that I'd made her laugh! I guess in a way it was my first ever performance and I liked the feeling that it gave me. It felt good to play the clown.

Not long after that I took the act to school, looking for opportunities to engage with the kids around me by making faces and messing around – anything to try to get a reaction. I thoroughly enjoyed my junior school days. Each new day was a fresh opportunity to play and engage and I loved being around the other kids. Looking back on it, I may have been disruptive; never maliciously so, but my lack of concentration certainly kept me out of the educational fast lane. I was just having fun, exploring and soaking everything in. I delighted in the sound of laughter and loved the sight of a smile. Any opportunity to stand up front was a chance to play around. Being rather quick on my feet, I found early wins in playground sprint races and always larked around when standing up at the front of the class to collect my medal. Always the clown and the kid with the smile, I wasn't that interested in learning. Of course, I knew that some of my classmates in different groups were covering more advanced subjects, but I didn't care. I always did just enough, knowing I wasn't the kind of kid that would set the place alight. I was just too busy having a good time. For me, life was simple: the streets were a little scary, home was fun and school seemed like the kind of place I was free to find my own way.

One day I was running around the playground pretending to be an aeroplane when:

'NEEEOOWW.'

Crash!

I bumped into this guy. And not just any guy but Godfrey Edwards, who was apparently considered one of the toughest kids in the school, something of a bad boy. I had no idea who this other Black boy was.

'Sorry,' I said.

But he came at me quickly and slapped me hard in the face. I remember everyone gathering round, ready for the coming fight, and the two of us circling and then in a flash . . .

I don't quite remember the play-by-play of what transpired next – it's all a blur – but by the time the teachers had pulled us apart I had seriously cut Godfrey across the top of his left eye and he was bleeding rather badly. I think everyone was genuinely surprised about how the fight went, including one of my teachers! He had a small smile on his face when he saw me sitting outside the headmaster's office, almost saying to me, 'Nice one!'

I was in a state of shock. Having been on the receiving end, I hated violence. This was the first time I'd ever actively participated in it. My heart was pounding and it took me a while to calm down as everything had happened so quickly. The feeling was unfamiliar: I'd always been the clown, not the fighter. But if I was ever to have walked a different path, it would have been around this time because there was a new awareness of me after the fight. I'd announced myself as a contender physically and there were different players in this game who eyed me up after that day. These tough guys were kids who didn't engage with the other kids in the class. They stayed on the periphery and seemed disinterested in being a part of the collective. And whilst I had enjoyed school, I had a sense that these kids were in a very different place. What I can see now is that for them, the school system had really become an extension of the 'white space'. It's as if those kids already understood that they'd struggle to find a future in it. In many ways these kids were more astute than me.

Meanwhile, I was busy taking in new information and soaking up whatever was put in front of me and assimilating quickly. I remember in particular a neighbourhood Black lady who would grab local Black kids on their way to school and comb their hair if she didn't think it was tidy enough.

'We have to always look our best here. You can't walk around looking like you don't care. Always look your best.'

I used to cross the road when I saw her. I was pretty quick on my feet so I could always outrun her if she came for me. But one day she wasn't where I expected her to be. I couldn't see her at all so, as I walked up the road, I began to relax. Suddenly, she sprang out from behind a fence and grabbed me! She dragged that comb through my hair hard. Back then, there were hardly had any products to moisturize Black hair and I didn't particularly care much about my appearance so, as she pulled that comb through my tight, nappy hair, she reprimanded me.

'Can't walk around lookin' like a John Crow.' (Sucking her teeth.) 'Must keep yourself tidy and clean here, understand? Look you best. Always!'

And then she let me go. I sulked away, chastened, she'd finally got me.

After the fight with Godfrey, it didn't take long for me to return to my natural clown self. In fact, the two of us became good friends shortly afterwards. My sense of humour and constant clowning helped me avoid further physical confrontation at junior school and I was glad of that. I didn't want any more trouble. That is when I really began to rely on my humour rather than my size and strength. One or two guys gave me a little grief over it, almost as if I was being too soft or 'too white', but I brushed it off. I wasn't interested in using my fists. I preferred to have a good time and go my own way but I guess it was an early sign that some Black kids weren't altogether convinced about me because I was different. I moved easily in the white space and enjoyed the friendships and company I kept, but I also understood that it made some Black kids unsure of me, even suspicious.

By now I was playing football quite regularly on a Saturday and Sunday and I was really happy when I found out a few of the team were set to attend the same secondary school as me, Washwood Heath Comprehensive in the Alum Rock area of the city. I was excited to go to secondary school. I remember putting my uniform on one evening a couple of days before I was due to start and checking myself out in Mum's full-length mirror. I put the whole damn uniform on, shoes, socks, trousers, shirt, tie, blazer; everything new, crisp and sharp. It looked awesome, another costume in which I could play the fool. I spent a few minutes taking it all in. Somehow, though, my reputation from the fight followed me to secondary school. On my first day at Washwood Heath on a mid-morning break I was standing with some friends outside the school gym when this white kid walked up to me and said: 'Your name Harewood?'

'Yes.'

'Outside. Three thirty.'

Back then that always meant a fight and although I was a little shocked that the boy seemed to know who I was, I nodded and said:

'Okay.'

And when the bell rang for the end of school I made my way towards the playing fields out the back, ready for whatever was to come. To my surprise, and I must say delight, the kid I was supposed to fight stopped me as I walked towards the fields and told me that just because I'd actually had the balls to turn up for the fight, it was enough to gain his respect.

'You're okay, Harewood,' he said and he walked off.

I'd dodged a bullet. I hated fighting and I really didn't want to be getting into it on my first day so this seemed like the perfect result. My reputation as somebody that could handle himself was intact without ever actually fighting at school full stop. Most of the toughest kids in the school were either my mates or had decided it wasn't worth the hassle fighting me. Luckily, at school, I never had to worry and was pretty well insulated from trouble, even enjoying some degree of respect amongst other kids.

My two elder brothers were at a different school: Cockshut Hill, a couple of miles away from Washwood. I never had a guiding hand throughout my school days from them and, although my sister also attended my school, I don't remember bumping into her that much. We each found our way with our own sets of friends. I remember my brother Paul, always a little mischievous, turning up one night when I was at home in this gorgeous Ford Capri that looked like it was out of a movie. I've no idea where he got it but he told me to jump in and took me for a wild ride round the streets of Small Heath! Heading home down the Coventry Road, he pulled on the hand brake and slid the car perfectly into Oldknow Road, just like the cars in the TV show *Dukes of Hazzard*, and pulled up outside the house to drop me off. It was the coolest thing I'd ever done. Each of us found our own ways into the white space, only we didn't think of it as white then. It was just the norm. All the teachers were white, we studied English history, listened to English pop music. I was now a Black teenager, listening to Ska music, obsessed with bands like The Specials and The Beat as they sung about and reflected my own world and expressed what I couldn't otherwise communicate.

My secondary school friends and I dominated the classroom. Kelly, Murphy, Parchment, Frenchie and Turner were my closest friends and my best mate of all was called Luigi. He was a handsome Italian lad and the two of us became inseparable, laughing every day and finding different ways to make nuisances of ourselves. Like my father, his dad worked on the railways and wore a similar uniform, too. He was a funny man, spoke broken English and Lui and I would often laugh at his pronunciation of some English words. Lui would ask him where he'd been working that day and he'd say:

'I work in eh, in eh, Fuck-es-ton.'

'Where, Dad?!'

'Fuck-es-ton!'

'Oh, you mean Folkestone!'

'That's what I say!!!'

The two of us would be cracking up! When I eventually told Lui that I was going to be an actor he was the only person who straight off the bat said:

'Brilliant, Dave! You're gonna be fantastic!'

He said it with such surety, almost like he knew it was going to happen. His faith in me always gave me such confidence. We'd spend hours together playing football or basketball or listening to whole albums in the front room of my house.

Because of my clowning, disruptive nature, I was quickly filtered into particular classes at Washwood Heath. I remember being aware that some of the classes I found myself in were full of the more disengaged students. Perhaps my behaviour had given me a 'disruptive' reputation, meaning I was liable to hold back others around me.

My friend Kelly and I sometimes played in the year above's first football team, and they ended up winning the All England Schools' Championship, a competition that took us all over the country. I was a goalkeeper, unusual for a Black kid then. They called me 'The Cat', as I was known for my spring-like reflexes, which came in handy as a shot-stopper. There were three or four older Black kids in the team. They were total legends and one of them went on to play for England schoolboys. I didn't quite have the confidence to clown around in that environment: these were serious dudes. I was shy. A couple of the stylish, cool Black lads were always surrounded by girls. A part of me felt I couldn't fall back on my joking ways around them because they were all so gifted athletically, and I wanted them to have confidence in me whenever I played.

We drew a team from Liverpool in the round of sixteen, a knockout game, and we travelled up on the coach that Saturday morning. It pissed down with rain all morning and, when our coach finally arrived in Liverpool, the rain had stopped but the skies were still dark and heavy. We were deep into an inner-city area: familiar enough, nothing too rough, decent houses, nice gardens. Finally, we pulled into the school. There was actually a little bit of a crowd and, as the coach slowed, the crowd began to circle it. The faces were angry, tribal; we were not expecting that. Descending from the coach, we were met with a barrage of the vilest racist abuse. It was terrifying and the venom in their voices took my breath away. They were apparently a very good team so we knew we were in for a tough game. The atmosphere was off the scale intimidating and the whole experience is fixed in my mind as an example of playing in a hostile environment. Don't get me wrong. I do love Scousers and have spent many a night in Liverpool on gigs over the years and always had a great time. They possess a natural gift with language and can be extremely witty and sharp, but this was next-level racism coming from families – mums and dads, kids and even teachers. A few of them crept round the back of my goal and spent the entire second half hurling the most awful stuff at me.

'Fuckin' Black cunt. Monkey bastard.'

For forty-five minutes, non-stop. We managed to get on top in the game and at half-time we were a goal up, but it was tight. Eventually we added a second goal whilst we did our best not to respond to the increasing abuse from the crowd and rough treatment from the other team. One of our best players, Paul Brown, who had scored the second goal, was brought down by a dreadful challenge from one of their players and he fell in a heap on the ground. It was such a shocking tackle that our manager, Mr Mortiboys, went running onto the pitch. He was an awesome teacher, deeply in tune with his players. I could see that he was finding the environment tough to deal with and when the tackle went in, he couldn't contain himself. Slipping in the mud as he set off which gave the others on the sideline time to grab him before he could get very far. I'd never experienced anything like it. I'd played in racist areas before, where it was best not to spend too much time after the game getting changed and hanging around, but on those occasions we'd just walk off the pitch and head straight for the bus. This was different, a relentless stream of intense verbal racist abuse lasting through the whole game. Looking back now, I don't ever remember talking about it with anyone afterwards. We may have seen the shock and fear in each other's eyes but there was never any discussion about what we'd experienced. This stunned silence is a feature of the Black experience in the UK, where we seem to have internalised our struggle for so long and our survival strategy is choosing not to speak. Some issues like mental health are often taboo in our community, as if we've somehow absorbed the British stiff upper lip culture, a culture of 'just get on with it'. There's even widespread denial that these experiences of racism exist. But I'm encouraged by the many older Black people who have approached me after *Psychosis and Me* aired to tell me:

'Young man. Just want to say well done. Very important you talk 'bout dem tings deh, bout mental health, very important. Nice, yeah. Well done.'

Speaking about my own struggle seems to have rung a bell for many Black people in the UK, giving them permission to talk and to acknowledge the pressures we are under that can break us. Things go wrong if you're not taking care of yourself and not sleeping or resting. I am genuinely astonished at the proportion of Black people in the mental health system in the UK. I have only recently discovered how overrepresented we are. In a way, knowing the context makes it all the more extraordinary that I managed to survive and go on to build a successful career. So many Black people suffer poor mental health as a result of the grind of surviving in a space that seems to act against you, undermining you, pushing you aside, sometimes unconsciously, making you feel as if you're living in a different reality. Rather than listen to what Black people have to say, they are shouted down, their experience is denied, and it becomes too exhausting to address the ignorance. This may be the most 'open and tolerant' country, but tolerance isn't enough when it comes to racism. People need to call it out or at the very least acknowledge its existence or we will be speaking with a completely separate set of facts. Being challenged on the existence of racism is tiresome, psychologically debilitating, and deeply depressing. I'm not surprised that so many of us break down living here in the UK.

Some people seem able to survive this horrific assault better than others. I have always had enormous respect for the professional Black footballers who emerged when I was in secondary school, the guys I'd watch of a Saturday night on *Match of the Day*. After my experience with the Leeds fans I knew how hostile that environment could be, so when I watched players like Cyrille Regis and Laurie Cunningham banging in the goals on a Saturday night I would marvel at their strength of character, understanding that they were playing at the top of their game despite the abuse they were undoubtedly getting from the terraces. I remember when Black English players started bursting onto the scene, like Mark Walters, bringing a flair to the English game. There was always a buzz whenever he got on the ball. He was a legend.

During the filming of Simon Frederick's excellent documentary *Black is the New Black*, which aired on the BBC in 2015, I actually met my own football hero, Cyrille Regis. Frederick sought to bring together Black British celebrities, musicians, sportsmen and women, and other famous Black personalities to detail their experiences growing up and working in the UK. It was powerful hearing each person describe the racism they'd had to overcome, despite their hard-earned fame. Once my interview was finished, I was sitting in a side room when Cyrille walked in. He must have seen the look on my face because he smiled straight away and walked forward to shake my hand. I felt like I was in the presence of royalty! The two of us chatted away and he let me know he'd seen a lot of my work, which was amazing to hear. I told him just how much it had meant to me as a kid, watching him play. I couldn't help asking him what it was like playing back in the '80s and how he'd coped with racism and his answer put a huge smile on my face.

'Made me wanna score even more, David!'

Hearing that filled me with joy. My boyhood hero used the abuse that terrified me as a child as fuel for his sport. Just like Popeye ate spinach, Cyrille took the abuse and turned it into raw power, pace and skill. I admire that and wish I had that strength. But not all Black people are built that way. We can't all walk through the fire without fear like Mr Regis and be at our supreme best under racist pressure, particularly in these days of social media and under the hot gaze of a hostile press. I marvel at our young Black footballers and sportsmen, Rashford, Sterling and Sir Lewis, standing strong in the face of online abuse and hostility and yet proud to wear the shirt and fly the flag. It's inspirational, something for me to work towards perhaps.

I hadn't fully understood exactly how growing up amidst racism had shaped my world. Black people make up around 3 per cent of the population in the UK and England's traditional culture and history dominates. I myself have benefitted from the rich and distinctive style of UK actors and comedians, which inspired me to 'play the clown'. But they were all white and back then I didn't give it a second thought. That's the dangerous thing about being a Black person in a white space: it works at a much deeper, unconscious level and it makes you feel as though everything you're taking in is normal – until it isn't. It's only when it isn't that you consider your 'otherness'.

I was a young teen now, beginning to have my eye turned by the opposite sex, and I was the first of my close friends to have a girlfriend. However, a couple of days after we decided that we would be an item, she came to school in tears and was surrounded by her friends as she tried to keep it together. I talked to her as soon as I could and learned that her father had found out that she was dating me and refused to allow it, demanding that she end the relationship immediately. She was pretty upset. I don't think she realised going out with a Black boy would create such a problem and, to be honest, neither did I. Her mother had told her to give it time, maybe her father would come round, but until he did we probably shouldn't be seen together. We both agreed and put the whole thing on ice.

A couple of weeks later she told me that her father wanted to talk to me 'mano-a-mano' and could I come to her house that evening. I did and was greeted at the door by her mother, who seemed pleasant. She stifled a smile and took me through to the kitchen and made me a cup of tea and as soon as it was on the table her father walked in. He was a short man, bespectacled, in a cardigan and slacks, and after introducing himself the two of us were left alone to talk. I think he must have been speaking for a couple of hours. I'm sure I had at least four cups of tea!

'It's just not right, you see, David. That's your name, isn't it?

David. Yes, I just don't see it as normal, you know what I mean? I think people should sort of stick to their own kind, like, you know, otherwise, all sorts of things could happen. I mean, I'm sure you're a nice lad. I watched you play football the other day and you seem very good. How long have you been a goalkeeper? Don't see many Bla . . . many Blac . . . you don't see many of your sort in goal. You lot are normally running around and stuff. Very unusual seeing someone like yourself in goal.'

This went on for what seemed like an eternity. I just listened to him, whilst he seemed to be reasoning it all out with himself because I didn't really know what to say. I spoke about football and how much I liked school, small talk mainly, but every now and again he asked me something about my family or where I lived. It was all very odd. He kept coming back to how it wasn't right that I should be seeing his daughter and I just kept nodding.

'Okay.'

After a while I thought I should be getting home so I made my excuses and said my goodbyes. His wife came into the kitchen and said goodnight and their daughter Julie popped her head round the kitchen door and said she'd see me at school and that was that. I remember travelling home on the bus in a real funk. Should I have tried to be more in his face? Did I fight my corner as well as I could have? I felt shit all the way home. It was the first time I'd experienced racism in a more personal, close-up way. It wasn't the kind of angry, nationalist racism shouted from a passing car or a direct threat from an angry skinhead; this was something altogether more polite and terribly British.

A couple of days later her father changed his mind, told her it was fine to see me. He thought I was okay, but even so, that evening stayed with me for some time afterwards. As usual, I didn't discuss it with friends and just kept it all to myself. Mum came home from bingo one night and found me on the sofa with Julie having a cuddle and after she left Mum gave me the birds and bees chat. Very awkward but she just wanted to make sure I was being safe. I remember my mates being pretty jealous that I had a girlfriend. They gave me some grief about it but I knew they were only pulling my leg. When they eventually had girlfriends, I would make them cassette mixes with appropriate 'slow jam' music on! By now my brothers had a pretty cool collection of records so I had plenty of tracks to choose from.

It was around this time that I was asked to be in my first school play. One of the teachers asked me if I could read a section of the Martin Luther King 'I Have a Dream' speech in a play he'd put together called *Illusions*, a collection of dream sequences that included an appearance of the great civil rights legend reciting his most famous speech, and I leaped at the chance to do it. I remembered seeing it on the TV as a child and I knew it was a very famous speech so I took it really seriously, learning it right away and attempting the accent too. I'm not sure the parents and kids who saw the show had ever seen anything like it! I remember being a little thrown on the first night because some of the Black parents in the audience were clapping and whooping as I delivered the speech. It was like being in a Baptist Church meeting! I walked off stage after that first show and my legs were shaking. It was a really powerful experience.

'Let freedom ring from the heightening Alleghenies of Pennsylvania.
Let freedom ring from the snow-capped Rockies of Colorado.
Let freedom ring from the curvaceous slopes of California.
But not only that, let freedom ring from Stone Mountain of Georgia.

Let freedom ring from Lookout Mountain of Tennessee.
Let freedom ring from every hill and molehill of Mississippi.
From every mountainside, let freedom ring.

And when this happens, and when we allow freedom to ring, when we let it ring from every village and every hamlet, from every state and every city, we will be able to speed up that day when all of God's children, Black men and white men, Jews and Gentiles, Protestants and Catholics, will be able to join hands and sing in the words of the old Negro spiritual: Free at last. Free at last. Thank God almighty, we are free at last.'

Wow. I had no idea what the 'snow-capped Rockies of Colorado' were but I just put everything into that speech and I loved the effect that it had on the audience. It was just the Black parents that were being vocal. They were completely into it and I remember really enjoying the feeling of being in front of an audience even though we only did five or six performances. Funny thing, though, on the second night there were no Black parents in the audience and the whole speech fell really flat, which kind of threw me. Second night performances always tend to throw you!

I guess I must have caught someone's eye because I was asked to be in another play the following year, Harold Brighouse's *Hobson's Choice*, in which I again put on a thick accent, this time northern for some reason, and had them rolling in the aisles with the line:

'To church? You can't do that!' With the 'that' pronounced very strongly! Sticking my tongue out to make the 'TH' sound before slamming down on the last syllable to make it sound like 'cat'.

I was basically mimicking our headmaster's accent. Luckily,

he thought it was hilarious and watched every single performance, laughing especially hard every time I said that line. After
the play was over he tried to give me a shoutout at the end of
morning assembly. I'd been a last-minute replacement in goal
for the 'all-star' year above football team that weekend and I'd
made one particularly 'cat-like' save that seemed impossible. We
ended up winning the game 1–0. I didn't know it was going to
happen but as he reached the end of his usual assembly shtick
he said:

'Before we depart this morning, I'd like to commend one particular pupil at this school for stepping up this weekend and playing
a vital role in securing the fifth-year boys' football team a place in
the quarter finals of the All England Schools' Championship. He
showed great courage in doing so and acquitted himself very well.
As he has done on the stage . . .'

Fuck! He's talking about me!

I turned to my mates and they were all smiles; even my teachers were chuffed. We all knew who he was talking about. But . . .

'And so, I'd like us all to put our hands together for David
Hellywell.'

Who?

There was a brief pause in the hall before someone started
clapping but it was too late, the moment had gone. He'd got my
name wrong and although I laughed it off, I was gutted. It was
such a simple thing but it ruined my day. I had a similar experience many years later at a launch event for season two of
Homeland in New York. I remember the event so well. Unlike
season one, I was more confident and settled in my performance. We were fresh winners of the Emmys and Golden
Globes and the network was splashing out on an elaborate
launch event, held on the USS *Intrepid*, a huge aircraft carrier

docked at Pier 86 in New York's Hell's Kitchen. It was a great night and after we'd all taken our seats David Nevin, the creative force behind Showtime, took the stage to welcome the attending glitterati to the very first reveal of the season two premiere.

He began by simply naming the cast and producers involved in the project but as soon as he started I had this sinking feeling, just like I did that day in assembly. He said:

'Ladies and gentlemen, I just want to start by thanking the extraordinary group of people who have brought this story to life, and captured the attention of so many people around the world. Alex Gansa. Howard Gordon. Gideon Raff. Michael Questa. Avi Nir. Ran Talem. Henry Bromell. Alexander Cary and Chip Johannessen.'

He was calling out the names of those involved in the show in this big former aircraft carrier, to give them their due in front of this gathering of the great and the good. But something in me remembered that moment in school when my headmaster had got my name wrong and I knew disaster was about to befall me again. After reeling out all the producers Nevin turned to the cast and continued.

'Complimented by an A-list cast. Claire Danes, Damian Lewis, Morena Baccarin, Mandy Patinkin, Diego Klattenhoff, Jackson Pace, Morgan Saylor.' By now he was already through the top half of the cast and he had completely forgotten to mention me. I think it was Damian and Claire who spoke up first; I heard them from the front shouting out my name and I stood and jokingly said:

'Oi! I think you're forgetting someone!'

David Nevin quickly corrected himself and I took a bow in front of the attending crowd in an awkward, funny moment but inside I was experiencing exactly the same emotions as I'd felt back then in school, embarrassment and feeling as if I was invisible.

I continued acting the next school year even though I didn't like the choice of play. I enjoyed the whole rehearsal process so much it was worth it staying behind after school to practise the scenes was fun. The social aspect of doing plays really appealed to me. I naturally enjoyed being around others and found the acting pretty straightforward: it was basically what I'd always been doing when I was messing around. I really didn't think there was anything to it. But I began to pay a little bit more attention in my English class when we studied *Othello* that year and marvelled with my mate Turner at the descriptive way Shakespeare wrote.

Iago: *I'll pour this pestilence into his ear: That she repeals him for her body's lust . . .*

Awesome! We both thought it was fantastic and I began to tune in to the language more and more. One day the teacher told us that we had an opportunity to go to the theatre to watch a Shakespeare play, *King Lear*. I was one of the first to raise my hand. Surprisingly, four of the worst-behaved lads in the class got to go on the trip and I remember riding to the theatre on the coach laughing with them. I fully expected to spend the evening messing around, but by the end of the play we were all fighting back tears. It blew us away. When the lights came up and the actors came on for their curtain call, I was really emotional. I'd never experienced anything like it and there was silence on the coach on the way back. I didn't think theatre could move me like that, and the evening made a huge impression on me.

With rehearsals and football taking up so much of my time, I was hardly ever home for long and if I was, I'd usually have either Lui or one of my other friends with me. The front room in our house became an entertainment hub where we would play games and listen to music, talk about girls and generally laugh till the early hours of the morning, only occasionally being asked to keep the noise down by one of my parents. Sometimes my mum would surprise my mates by popping her head around the door to the front room to ask if anybody was hungry or needed a drink, and she would often make everyone a big plate of chips and endless cups of tea.

'Your mum's great, Dave,' Lui would say as he filled his face with food.

'These are bostin' chips!'

There weren't many other places we could all be together and hang out like we did at my house. I have to credit my parents for being so welcoming. Our doors were always open and whether it was me or my brothers or sister, my mum made sure that all were welcome. I remember being quite proud of that.

Chapter Four

Things Fall Apart

My father and I were both popular amongst our peers. I'd become something of an entertainer in the classroom and was forever playing team sports whilst my father had become quite a handy darts player, creating a league of different local pub teams who played each other on a weekly basis. It absolutely took off. He collated all the results of the different games and gave each match a little write-up, noting who beat who, by what score. Then he'd type up all the information on his little typewriter and deliver it to the local paper just in time for the weekend's games. He designed a logo for the league and, at the end of every season, organised an awards evening where folks from all the pubs in the area who had taken part would come to drink and celebrate the seasons' achievements. He handed out trophies, introduced guests and a lot of the money raised went to charity. I was proud of him being the master of ceremonies during those evenings, although he did sometimes go on a bit! Like me, he had lots of friends, trophies and medals – his for the darts, mine for the football and athletics.

I was into my early teens now and I was hardly ever home for dinner as I'd be out playing sport or fooling around with my mates.

Perhaps that's why I missed the first signs of what was happening with my father, but I began to sense that all wasn't well. For a couple of mornings I didn't hear him jingle jangle down the stairs. And Mum told me not to go into the kitchen when I went downstairs. She said I should get ready and head straight out the door to school. I started to suspect that something wasn't quite right. Everybody loved my father, but maybe we didn't understand the strain he was putting himself under with all his work. He was forever on that typewriter, writing down the names of pubs and different players.

The Marlborough Arms beat The Brewer and Baker.
Sullivan played well, beating Taylor 3–1 in the best of 5.
Harborne beat Lewis 3–0.
Smith came from behind in a classic, to beat
Marshall 3–2.
The Marlborough Arms will be through to the semi-final
if The Crown and Anchor fail to beat The Fox and Grapes.

He was incredibly detailed with his work and he would type away into the evening making sure everything was in order. One evening I came home from a late night and walked in to find all the lights on in the house but nobody downstairs. I figured someone had forgotten to turn them off so I sat for a minute, taking in the living room, pondering whether or not to turn on the TV, when my eyes fell on my father's typewriter. It had a single piece of paper in it and for some reason something just looked off. I walked up to it. It was like a scene straight out of Stephen King's *The Shining*. There was only one word typed on a whole sheet of A4 paper and it said:

Illness

It was then that I understood. My father wasn't well – something had happened; something in his mind had cracked. My sister tells me that the family had decided to shield me because I was the youngest. Eventually, my father was sectioned. He was in the hospital for quite some time and he hated every damn minute of it. We went to see him once with the whole family travelling up to sit with him one evening whilst he spoke quietly with my mother. I could tell he really wasn't happy, because he was grouchy and snapped at my mother from time to time. I sat watching him, not really understanding what was going on but knowing that he had been 'detained', and that he had to stay there until the doctors thought he was better. I wasn't thrown by the surroundings. In fact, I was relatively relaxed. At one point a security guard asked for my brother's ID because he didn't think he was old enough to be sitting where we were and my brother got upset because I was younger than he was and the guard hadn't bothered me. Maybe I was taking it all in, and maybe that's why I wasn't so thrown, myself, when I woke up in a mental institution some years later.

I must have been quite wrapped up in my own world then because I wasn't very aware of my father's breakdown. When I had my breakdown it was out in the open but when my dad was struggling, I guess everyone in the family did a good job of protecting me from the worst of it. Although I do remember seeing him in the psychiatric ward and he looked different, unhappy, and like he was being kept against his will. He was a proud man and I think he found it humiliating to be hospitalised for his mental health. I choose to look at being sectioned another way. I'm not at all embarrassed about what happened to me. In truth, before it went horribly wrong there were moments when it felt as though I was going through some kind of shamanic experience with the most extraordinary energy flowing through me. I know in some ways I was lucky to have the experience that I did. Everyone's psychosis is different and particular to them alone; it can manifest in a multitude of ways.

Coming from the Caribbean and arriving in England must have also been a shock to my father's system. And when I was filming *Psychosis and Me*, I was so battered by what I discovered about my own experience that I really didn't have the bandwidth to speak of my father's as well. Now I've had more time to digest what happened, I can see the close connection and its importance more clearly. Within ten years of each other, we would both be having mental health problems.

While it is impossible for me to ever truly understand what made my father snap, if I follow my own journey into madness, maybe I can shed some light on his struggles and finally understand what landed him in the Connally Psychiatric Hospital several years before my own crisis. My father had left what he knew in Barbados to come to England and then had a breakdown. I had left the life I knew to become an actor and also suffered a breakdown. The white space had taken its toll on both of us.

When he got out of the psychiatric ward my father was a very different man. Mental illness can have a profound effect on a person's life and personality and many people experience a big change after going through a breakdown. My father was bitter, angry at the system – in particular the doctors and the nurses for thinking he was crazy – and he was angry at those who didn't see things the way he'd seen them.

'The neighbours should have let me park my truck on the street.'

'Just a couple of stupid people, you know. Just tell them to bugger off.'

'How come I'm using all my own money to buy these trophies for the darts league? And why isn't anybody stepping up with ideas?'

'Why did Mayleen call the authorities? I was fine?'

Years of resentment finally rising to the top and exploding out in a volcanic eruption of mental activity.

Breaking down is a shattering experience, one where your mind plays tricks on you and your thoughts run away, leaving you unable to tell the difference between what's real and what isn't. Some sufferers remain in denial for years, refusing to accept what has happened. I just buried all the pain and confusion that led to my own breakdown, buried it so deep that I totally forgot it was there and just carried on with life. It was only the documentary that brought it back to my full attention, which is why it was so shocking and distressing to encounter it all again. Maybe I needed to examine it. Although it was painful, bringing it all out into the open was probably the right thing for me to do.

My father, on the other hand, ruminated on his breakdown and never forgot it, blaming my mother for his being sectioned and holding it against her for the rest of their marriage. In the months and years following, they argued more than they ever had before. The house wasn't filled with much laughter. Dad threw himself into his darts and activities down the pub, drinking heavily and often becoming a little belligerent. He wasn't the same dad that I remembered and after a while everyone in the house felt the same way. It was like he'd replaced the man he used to be with the man he'd decided to be and that person was different.

He was diagnosed with hypermania – whatever that meant, I wasn't sure. Nobody really gave us any explanations. He was told to take lithium tablets which would help keep him on an even keel, but he decided he didn't need them. Nobody had any answers as to why it had happened and the atmosphere in the house was never the same again. I was fifteen years old and my world had completely changed. How had it come to this? Just three or four years earlier, I'd been sitting with my father watching the cricket. My father became yet another Black man who had malfunctioned in England, short-circuited, and was in need of repair. It was something that I hadn't foreseen, but then I guess this kind of trauma never is.

Looking back, I can recognise that there may have been some alcohol abuse and stress with the darts league, but my father was a strong man. I'm not sure what made him step off the deep end. Perhaps I should have taken more notice that if this could happen to someone in the family and someone who seemed so strong, it might also happen to me. Maybe I should have paid more attention.

According to the 2019–20 NHS Mental Health Act, Black and minority people suffer elevated rates of psychosis and schizophrenia compared with white people in the UK, and a far higher rate than Black people of a similar age in the Caribbean. Of course, there are no easy answers but I would hazard a guess that socio-environmental factors play a role. When I think about it, I'm not surprised at all. White British culture can be deceiving. It can make you feel like you belong and that everything is normal. But if you don't consciously monitor your thoughts and experiences carefully, every single resentment you've ever had, every single rejection, all the stress and hard paddling you've done can build up and break you, leaving you a shell of yourself, relying on tablets to keep yourself together.

My father never really recovered from going to hospital. He chose not to take his medicine when he left and continued to drink heavily. I could hear muffled arguments between him and my mother through the wall of my bedroom and there were more and more disagreements.

The next stage arrived earlier than I expected when my parents told us they were getting divorced. My father was going to move out and the rest of us were going to be living at the house without him. I didn't quite know how to feel about the family splitting up. We'd spent our whole lives together and now something was broken and falling apart, but I had to acknowledge that my father was a changed man. Perhaps it was best that he move on? All seemed set when suddenly I was told exactly the opposite. My mum was moving out and taking my sister with her and I was to stay with my father and brothers in the house. That came as a blow. I really wasn't expecting that. I'd almost got used to the idea of my dad leaving and had made my peace with it, but losing my mum made the whole thing much more painful.

It cut me up when Mum left. Without her guiding hands looking after me, I drifted. I missed her presence and our old life, especially at Christmas. I used to love family Christmases, all the food and the presents and Christmas telly we'd watch together. Suddenly I was going to two houses on Christmas Day, and I didn't feel settled in either of them. Neither house felt like home. For the first time I didn't quite belong even at home. My foundations were rocked. My father was now a distant presence, hardly talking and keeping his own counsel most of the time. He was still caring and made sure we were looked after but the place just wasn't the same anymore.

I tried not to show how upset I was after my mum and sister moved out, but it really broke me up. One afternoon I was home from school and the doorbell rang. I opened it and there was my mother. She wasn't expected and I was startled to see her. As I let her in, I asked:

'Why didn't you use your key?'

She said:

'I don't live here anymore.'

It tore me up inside. We talked for a while and she did her usual thing of reassuring me and asking if I was okay. I tried my best to keep it together but I'm not sure I did a particularly good job. She had to go and made her way to the door, picked up her handbag and left. I walked back into the living room, collapsed and began sobbing like a child. Wouldn't you know it, Mum used her key, opened the door, came straight up to me and gave me the biggest hug you could imagine, and I stayed buried in her arms for quite some time. I was so glad she did that. I don't quite know what would have happened if she hadn't.

Suddenly childhood was over. Everything was different. Although I continued to play the clown at school, I wasn't the same person back at home. And the days at my safe space of school were running out and I had absolutely no idea what I wanted to do with my life. My eldest brother was thinking about doing a culinary course (even though I'd never seen him cook an egg) and my other brother Paul was running wild getting up to mischief with his friends. Without the audience of my classmates, I wasn't really sure what else I wanted to do. School had been my everything. But, out of the blue one afternoon, I got a phone call that would completely change the direction of my life.

Chapter Five

'A' For Actor

Moving into sixth form, I opted to stay on and do my A-levels rather than leave and find a job. Most of the lads around me did the same. We completed the first term of sixth form when Lui was kicked out of school because he had slacked on the academics. It was a bit of a shock to us. He was my best mate and I didn't really know how I was going to get through the rest of my time there without my comedy wing man next to me. But Lui was resourceful. He got a job almost immediately and, to everyone's delight, the job also came with a company car. He would pick us up in the evenings after school and take us all over town as we drank cider in the back and cruised around the city. We were getting older now and with Lui working it seemed as if we were all moving into a different stage of our lives.

It was around this time that Lui came to my house and asked me if I wanted to come with him to work at Albert's, this wine bar in the city centre where his sister worked. Lui had been working there a couple of nights a week and they needed another pair of hands to help out. I jumped at the chance – anything to get away from the house was cool with me – and so I met Lui in town and together we walked over to the bar.

'The guy who owns this place can be a bit scary, Dave, don't nick anything!' Lui told me.

Albert's was in a beautiful Victorian building in the Dale End area of town and it covered two buildings on Albert Street, a top room and a main room that served wine and food and catered to an affluent crowd: a blend of local officials and management from the nearby stores in the day and, by night, different characters, ordering champagne and drinking heavily. Lui and I were running around collecting glasses and stocking the fridges with wine and champagne and generally helping out wherever we were needed, sometimes going round the front of the bar to serve customers. It was the first time I'd handled money and observed people in an environment like that. It really was a very exciting time. I only worked there a couple of nights at first but, within two or three months, Lui and I were basically full-time staff, sometimes even locking up at night and opening up the next day.

The place was owned by Colin, who I imagined to be a real Tony Soprano type. Loved and feared in equal measure, he dominated the bar whenever he was in and attracted a collection of 'Goodfellas' to the bar every night. These were guys in sharp suits and cool clothes, some with dolly birds on their arm and others with loyal wives. They always stood at the corner of the bar, drinking and occasionally popping into the kitchen for a quick line of cocaine. I was seventeen years old and the whole thing was eye-opening. I loved it. I couldn't wait to get to work when I got home from school. Alongside Colin was his wife Hilary, a real rock of a woman. Anyone who could live with Colin had to be, but she had real class. I admired her and she would sometimes help me with my homework on quiet nights at the bar and be attentive to my schooling. She became a great presence in my life over this period and I began to spend more time at the bar than I did at home. I couldn't get enough of the place and it started to feel more like home than my actual home.

I'm not sure if any of the regulars that frequented the bar had actual jobs but there was always money about and the champagne would be flowing on Friday and Saturday nights. Normally we wouldn't leave the bar till gone three or four in the morning. We used to have legendary lock-ins, once all the punters were gone. We'd put the music back on and settle in for a long night of drinking and raucous laughter. I used to love listening to the stories these guys told whenever any of them had a new tale to tell. After being there a while, I suggested that my brother, who was now a DJ, play the odd night over a weekend and Colin agreed to give him a go. Paul played a couple of weekends and was an instant hit and played every weekend in there for the following two years. I even got my mum a job there as a cleaner. I was there pretty much every night of the week and at weekends either playing music I'd made at home on the wine bar's own system or listening to my brother spin the tunes and watching the customers dance on the tables.

As Lui could drive, every now and again one of Colin's mates would ask him to bring their cars round to the front. We'd both head out the back door looking for a Jag or BMW or a Merc, find it, jump in and cruise round to the front of the bar past all the girls, parking perfectly. As I didn't drive, I always played it as if I was head of security, watching Lui's back should anyone get any ideas. We worked really well together. Well, I say work, but Lui would always go missing on a busy night and with a packed bar. You'd soon notice if you were a man down. Colin would tell me to go and find him and after a brief look around I'd usually find him with his tongue down some girl's throat, kissing passionately, completely oblivious to the world around him.

'Lui! Colin's looking for you.'

'Shit. Sorry, Dave.'

He was a handsome bugger! Tall and strong and funny to boot, he was a great hit with the opposite sex and always seemed to have options when it came to deciding which lucky lady he'd be heading home with. He had extraordinary confidence and I was quite in awe of his ability to get women to respond and follow his lead. In contrast, I was always quite shy around girls. We made a funny pairing but complemented each other well, which could be very entertaining.

Colin had been known over the years as a bit of a wild one but he really took Lui and me under his wing. His protection allowed us into a world of late-night drinking and laughter, characters and girls. When I started at the bar, there were one or two Black people that came there, but with my brother and me working there, more and more Black people felt comfortable as customers. The previously white space had become more populated with other Black faces and it seemed a good thing.

I missed being with Lui at school in the daytime, but we made up for it by spending as much time together in the evenings as we could, working or hanging out at my place listening to music. I was heading for my final exams now and my days at Washwood Heath were very nearly over. Time had slipped away and suddenly we were the oldest kids in the school and into the last stretch. I remember sitting in my history exam and turning my paper over to read the questions and being hit with the reality that I couldn't answer any of them particularly well. When I turned round to have a laugh with a couple of lads behind me, I saw them all writing, busy getting on and applying themselves. That was the moment I realised the fun was over. I was on my own and I had to start thinking about what I was going to do. I started writing some old shit and hoped for the best.

By now I'd had a few football trials and an England schoolboy trial but football wasn't really in my blood. I enjoyed it but that wasn't what I wanted to do. I was at a loss. I'd spent all my time at school clowning around and not given much thought to my future. Although some of my mates were off to university and others into jobs, nothing was really appealing to me. I spent hours in the school careers library flicking through musty old pamphlets about various vocations but it all sounded so dull; absolutely nothing seemed to excite me. I worried for a while that I'd be leaving with nothing to go on to. Then one day I was at home alone when the phone rang and, when I answered it, it was my English teacher Mr Reader, asking me if I'd come into the school as he had something he wanted to say to me that he didn't want to say over the phone. I was intrigued and said I'd be on my way and when I arrived we spoke for about five minutes – five minutes that totally changed my life. I remember it so clearly. If I listen closely, I can still hear him say:

'David. What are you going to do when you leave school?'

I had no idea so I said: 'Don't know, sir.'

'Well, we've all been chatting in the staffroom today and . . . we think you should be an actor.'

If ever there was a eureka moment in my life, that was it. I paused for just one second and then was suddenly filled with a passion, verve and spirit that are still here this very day. I went home that night knowing for the first time what I wanted to do with my life. It was almost as though I'd been given permission to go and fulfil my dreams, even though I didn't know anything about the business of acting. My teacher had given me direction, something to aim at and I wasn't about to let this opportunity pass. I was going to be an actor! Now all I had to do was work out how to go about it.

'We think you should be an actor.'

Wow. That's what my teacher had said. I was absolutely buzzing! I didn't know how I was going to make it happen, but I knew I had enough energy and purpose about me to find out. I had five weeks left at school, so I had to act fast to use the school's resources and get support from Mr Reader. He ran his eye over the first letters I wrote to local theatre groups asking for any information on courses and workshops. Within a couple of days I'd received various pamphlets and brochures on courses and dates of entry. None of it really spoke to me and after throwing a couple of ideas around, we thought about the Birmingham Youth Theatre. I wrote them a letter that Mr Reader looked over, to see if they had any openings in their youth group. Nothing doing. So we moved on to the following one on the list which was the National Youth Theatre. They were conducting regional auditions and ran a course every summer in London that lasted for five to six weeks and involved working on a text and playing with different groups. I thought that sounded cool so I wrote off to them and after a couple of weeks I had an audition set up.

I remembered *Othello* from school. It was the only play I really knew but I didn't want to do the obvious take on it and trot out an *Othello* speech. I thought it would be more interesting to do Iago instead and purposely not do the Black character, instead choosing the Machiavellian other. My approach worked. A week or so later I got a letter at home telling me I'd been accepted on the course. I was taking my first steps into the world of acting and actually heading down to London.

I'd been working in the library now for the last four weeks. I had already spent a lot of time in there over the last year, sifting through all the vocations in the 'jobs' section from A to Z trying to find a direction but I never did. Just in case anybody wished to follow in my footsteps, the school asked me to put all of the information I'd collected from the various drama groups and acting classes I'd written to. I created a whole new entry:

'A' for Actor.

I was excited about being away from home. When I told Mum and Dad of my plans to head to London and join the NYT, they were both initially surprised but my dad was particularly unsure. Maybe they thought it was some kind of phase I was going through. But I was determined and full of passion for it.

One night I came home from the bar quite late and flicked the telly on. I got immediately caught up in this movie that was showing. I'd just missed the beginning and didn't know what it was but I recognised a few of the actors and so I thought I'd see what was going on and it turned out to be the 1957 classic movie *12 Angry Men*, directed by Sidney Lumet. One of the things that makes the film so remarkable is that it all takes place in one room. Henry Fonda is the only juror who believes the defendant may be innocent and he's confronted with twelve angry jurors who aren't prepared to even talk about anything other than a 'guilty' decision. It's a wonderful film. By the end Fonda convinces all twelve to change their pleas, but it's a constant battle of wills and the acting is first class. I watched the film intently till the credits rolled then turned the telly off and just sat there stunned. I'd never seen anything like it: no car chases, no action sequences, or exterior shots of any kind, just pure dialogue and brilliant acting. I had to check the *TV Times* to make sure I knew what the film was, and it remains one of my favourite movies of all time. I went to bed that night inspired by what I'd seen. I thought to myself, *I want to do stuff like that.*

If only I knew then that years later I'd be living in New York doing a play, and one night after the show I'd go to a party and see a guy on a bar stool drinking alone and recognise him straight away as Sidney Lumet! I couldn't help it. I walked up to him and introduced myself. I told him how instrumental his film had been in my decision to become an actor, how the performances had inspired me. He was genuinely delighted. And told me of the battles he'd had with the studio about the script, how they didn't believe it could be shot in just one room. They wanted changes but he fought for the idea. However, when he was shooting he realised that they'd had a point! It looked like the same room on camera so they decided to build the set in accordance with the shot. Sometimes they would lower the ceiling or cheat a wall closer than it should have been and use lighting to create different shapes. It was a fascinating encounter, and I could hardly believe that there I was with the director of the film that had lit me up all those years earlier.

Seeing that film weeks before I was to go away on my first ever overnight trip to London felt like a sign. This was what I wanted to do.

Chapter Six

An Actor's Life For Me

W hat would I say to my younger self that night after watching *12 Angry Men*, weeks away from starting out on my
decades-long journey into the world of acting? What advice
would I holla at the young Black boy? That's a hard one. I'm not
sure I'd have listened, but I would have tried to instill a sense of
value in him, to remind him he had worth and the power to say
'no'. There's not much else I'd change because I was about to start
having the time of my life.

Summer of 1983 in London! The big city. I'd be staying at my
Aunty Yvonne's flat in Paddington in her spare room; she'd put
her young son Peter in with her whilst I took the room. She was a
real character and very different from my mother, more relaxed
and a little on the naughty side. She worked through most nights
cleaning offices in the city centre, but she had a number of side
moves going on. She had parties every other weekend that
summer and although the flat was tiny, there must have been over
a hundred people drifting through the place over the course of a
night. First thing in the morning it would start: the guys would
arrive and move all the furniture out of the lounge and store it in

the bedroom. Meanwhile you'd see these huge bass speakers being carried in by four or five guys, manoeuvred around the front door and tucked into the corners of the room. The smell of rum filled the place and silver-haired dreads smoked weed in the kitchen, talking in hushed tones. I'd head out for the day for the course and come back at night and hear the music from a block away! There were people all around drinking booze, enjoying the summer vibes and eating hard food from paper plates. Winding up the stairs of the building, lovers kissed in all small spaces and others drew on blunts. I made my way closer to the music and slipped into the flat, unrecognisable in the pitch black, with countless shapes in the dark moving closely, hardly dancing, swaying to the pounding bass. It was a hell of an introduction to the city and it suited me just fine!

I had a great time at the NYT and from the moment I arrived I knew I'd found the right people. I'd been messing around all my life but here with these other players and actors, I'd found my tribe. Looking back on it, I think I was the only Black person in my year group but because I was used to that I wasn't inhibited and thoroughly enjoyed myself throughout the course. I realise that my colour was hardly ever mentioned and that summer once again I found myself in the white space. But within the space – like at school – I could do or be anybody I chose to be. I really thrived in this new environment. Over the course of the five weeks we did exercises throughout the day, in groups or pairs, working on ideas and presenting them back to the group. As the weeks passed, we linked the better ideas into some kind of performance in front of an audience to complete our term. It was great. I loved every single day, making my way around the old bridge that led from the station, up and over Bishop's Bridge and over to Dudley House. It's gone now, buried under mountains of money and glass. But it was a home away from home back then. I was travelling on the London Underground every day, switching lines from Circle to District, Metropolitan and Bakerloo. Yellow, Green, Purple, Brown, the colours of the lines to get me home of an evening, though it was always best not to leave it too late. I remember one particularly long day; I'd had something of a breakthrough during an improvisation. The premise was that my wife had died, and I wanted to find out what had happened, but my acting partner was playing a very bureaucratic official. The two of us stood up in the middle of the group of about twenty kids and started the exercise. He was brilliant and gave me dry, posh, English dismissiveness. He was curt and formal and I found myself suddenly angry and emotional. And then he hit me with this line:

'Well . . . worse things happen at sea.'

I just flipped. From nowhere I found this whole speech about my family and how much they meant to me and how much I loved them and with every new 'love' I pushed him physically across the space. Basically I physicalised my emotions. I didn't hurt him but it was a strong push that I kept repeating and it ended up being a really powerful and emotional piece. It was the first time I'd ever experienced something like that, getting emotional in an artificial setting. There'd been that time when my knees shook after the Martin Luther King speech, but this was different. It surprised me. The piece was really well received and seemed to lift the whole group, everyone was buzzing afterwards and at the end of the day we all headed to a nearby pub to get some drinks. There were about sixteen of us there, all drinking and laughing and sharing stories when I suddenly started slowly drumming a beat on the table, which everybody picked up. And as I conducted them, I launched into song! For some crazy reason I'd memorised the lyrics of the old 1961 Jimmy Dean song 'Big Bad John'. My parents had a copy of the track on vinyl in their collection and as a child I'd fallen in love with the story it told of Big Bad John and what he did down the mine. I'd heard it played so many times I'd learned it and it just came out of me! I knew all the lyrics and directed the drumbeat on the tables as everybody leaned in and joined in the chorus.

It was one of the funniest things I'd ever done and it went down an absolute storm. I remember thinking that night that I really enjoyed being around creative people, and if this was what being an actor was about, then I was all in. We stayed in the bar till very late and only just managed to grab our trains home. It had been a great day and we all laughed as we said our goodnights. I headed down to get my train and managed to get halfway home when I struck up a half-drunken chat with a girl who had sat down next to me on the bench as we were waiting for the next train. We chatted for a while; she was a white girl, pretty, seemed very interested in the fact that I was acting and that it was my first time in London. All was going well when over the announcement system a voice told us that the last train had been cancelled and the station was now closing. There were grumbles all around. I was a bit worried because I didn't really know my way back to where I was staying. The girl I'd been talking to was also looking unsure of what to do. She was heading back to her boyfriend's for the night. Everyone was trying to work out what their next move should be so I asked her:

'Where are you headed?'

'I'm staying at my boyfriend's in Paddington,' she said.

'I live in Paddington, but I don't know the way from here. But if you know how to walk in the general direction of Paddington, I could walk you to your boyfriend's and find my way from there?'

She said she'd have to call her boyfriend and just let him know the situation as he'd be worried and it was going to take us about twenty-five minutes. We headed for a phone box. She was tall and striking and as she stood in the light of the phone box I watched her, observing as she played with her hair. When she was finished on the phone she pushed open the door.

'Come on then, Mr Actor.'

We headed off into the London night and we didn't stop talking the whole way. She was lovely and we had this strange, playful chat as we walked through the hot, London night. Turns out she'd always wanted to go into acting but had opted for a more regular, predictable life instead. She seemed a bit sad about it. After fifteen minutes, I began to get my bearings. We were heading to the posher end of Paddington, close to where I was staying but a lot more well to do. I remember joking with her that it was so posh she'd have to look after *me* should anyone see a Black man in the vicinity and call the police. At one point we cut through an alley, not pitch black but with dark shadows. When we emerged I told her that she'd been incredibly trusting, and that I hoped she didn't always do this! She laughed.

'I feel very safe with you, like *very* safe. I don't know why. I feel like I've known you for ages. You're a very old soul.'

I was still high from the fabulous day I'd had and here I was topping it off by walking through London with a beautiful girl I'd only just met. It seemed like the perfect end to a perfect day. It was all just fun and I kept it quite light. Soon enough we were on her boyfriend's road. The houses were huge and all painted white. I hadn't been to this part of town before and standing in one doorway was a guy, dressed in a T-shirt and tracksuit bottoms, and when he saw us he ran down towards us and immediately gave her a hug. By then I'd already said goodbye, didn't want it to get awkward. I bro-nodded to him as I turned and walked away. But from behind me I heard:

'Excuse me, young man. Hello.'

He ran up to me and grabbed my hand to shake it vigorously.

'Thank you so much for walking her home. I really appreciate you doing that. Thank you very much.'

He was quite posh.

I nodded. 'No problem.'

The two of them walked into the flat waving as they said goodnight. What a day! I felt like I was falling in love with the city that night. Meeting all these new people, chatting to strangers, observing the sights and sounds, it was intoxicating. My life was moving in a new and exciting direction.

A couple of days later, I was approached by the man who ran the National Youth Theatre, Michael Croft, a larger-than-life guy who had been watching the day's classes. Michael took me aside and asked for a chat. He was the top guy but I wasn't intimidated because I was having too much of a good time to worry about what he might think. I remember him telling me that he thought I was very good. It was the first time anybody with professional experience in acting had given me a compliment like that, and I was a little thrown. He could obviously see that by the look on my face because he chuckled.

'You are! You've got a lot of presence and I've been asking around and everybody seems to like your company very much. In fact, I wanted to ask you if you'd like to come back next year? We're doing *As You Like It* in Regent's Park at the open-air theatre.'

I was so chuffed. 'Absolutely! Thank you!'

'Keep it under your hat for now but I'd very much like you to be with us next year,' he said.

Because I'd been asked not to speak about coming back to the other students, I kept it low profile but I was flying for the remaining weeks of the course. When it was finally over, our group had bonded so tightly that there were actual tears when we parted ways. I'd never experienced that level of camaraderie and it would become one of the most joyous and wonderful aspects of working as an actor. Over the years, I've made intense and all-consuming friendships, only for them to be over in an instant and us never to be together again.

Heading home on the train back to Birmingham, I felt like I'd grown up and had my first experience of the big wide world. I had loved it so much that I was a little nervous about getting back to my old life, but because I'd been invited back the following year, I had something to hold on to. Mum and Dad were happy that I'd had a good time and everyone at the wine bar was delighted to have me back and proud that it seemed to have gone well. I even remember all the 'Goodfellas' giving me a round of applause when I walked back into the bar a couple of nights later. They were genuinely happy for me and the fact that I'd been asked back was proof that I'd made my mark. Colin had such a smile on his face. He wanted to know all about the course and I had to debrief him in the kitchen that night. During lock-ins that followed, I began doing my audition pieces behind the bar, reciting Shakespeare to all the people that had stayed for the after-hours drinks. They were amazed. Some of them hadn't heard Shakespeare since school. They'd ask me about the odd language and thought it was crazy that I knew what it meant. Sometimes I'd follow the speeches with impersonations. My impression of Colin was always particularly well received. I don't think he'd ever seen anything like it. I had all his mannerisms, how he used to move and drill the bar with his hand when he was thinking. Everyone was laughing so hard. I'd grown in confidence from doing the course and there was more of an ease about me.

Lui was really excited I'd found acting and never had a moment's doubt about my talent. I didn't know if I could be in the business for real but Lui was sure of it.

'You're gonna be big, Dave. I just know it,' he said.

I went back to the NYT the following year and played Charles the court wrestler in *As You Like It*, only rather than wrestle we worked out a whole boxing match that two of us choreographed along with our fight director Terry King, who would eventually be my fight director at drama school. I really enjoyed learning all the techniques. I'd always been physical so I took to this aspect of the craft very quickly. It was my first ever proper play and I'll never forget that feeling of being backstage when the audience was coming in and taking their seats. I spied through a hole in the set as the theatre filled up and the sun set just beyond in the distance. I knew at that moment without a doubt that this was what I wanted to do for the rest of my life. The cast members, all different types of people – some working class, others quite posh – had bonded closely and after the show every night the drinks would flow and the laughter was raucous. I was having the time of my life. There was an actor who played the melancholic Jaques who gives the amazing 'All the World's a Stage' speech and I would creep round to the side and watch from the wings as he delivered it every night. I was still new to Shakespeare. We'd read a little in our English class and I'd seen *King Lear*, but this experience really piqued my attention. How could somebody write like that, with such poetry, beauty and meaning? I was transported when I heard it and playing Jaques, this guy had the audience in the palm of his hands.

> *All the world's a stage,*
> *And all the men and women merely players;*

They have their exits and their entrances;
And one man in his time plays many parts

I thought to myself:

One day I'm going to be playing parts like that.

After the play one evening I was talking with the director and he advised me to go to drama school. I didn't really know what he was talking about so he explained that by going to drama school I could get formal training for my body and voice and learn more about the craft of acting. It sounded great so when I returned to Birmingham, I grabbed a *Yellow Pages* and began writing down the addresses of all the drama schools in London. Because I didn't know one from the other the list wasn't in any order. I just took down the addresses and started writing off to them for details about their courses. After a short while I started getting responses, dates for auditions and prospectuses, information about the schools and all the fluff about being a student at that institution. I filled out the required paperwork and waited.

I'd finished school by now, so I'd wake up and head downstairs to peek into the front room to see if there was any post for me on the floor underneath the letter box. My excitement was building as this was the first time official-looking letters were arriving addressed to me.

My first couple of auditions didn't go so well! Not that I was rubbish, but it was the first time I had spent a whole day audition-ing rather than just doing a single speech. I was surprised that the auditions involved a workshop with other participants running through a number of exercises. I became totally distracted in my first audition because I began messing around with this girl who, like me, wasn't really familiar with the process. At the end of the audition I knew it hadn't gone very well so I wasn't surprised when a week later I got a thin letter from the school telling me I hadn't been successful. I just went to the next school on the list, Mountview Academy. Again, I travelled down to London on my free rail pass to do my thing. I was prepped this time and enjoyed working with the other young actors. I left feeling good about what I'd done and, lo and behold, a week later a big, thick envelope arrived. I was accepted! The package contained lots of information about the classes and the history of the school and even details of where to live. I was really happy about getting in and so I cancelled all the remaining auditions, informing the schools that I'd been accepted on a course. As far as I was concerned, each drama school was as good as the other so why not cancel them? Nobody was guiding me through this process and I had next to no information. Little did I know, I had actually cancelled all the top drama schools in the country, including RADA, Central School of Speech and Drama, LAMDA, Drama Centre and Guildhall.

I skipped into the wine bar that weekend keen to tell everyone my news and the first person I saw was Hilary, Colin's wife. I told her what had happened.

'That's good, love. What's the place called?' she said.

'Mountview,' I replied.

'Shame it's not RADA. But well done, you!'

I remember that stinging a little. RADA? Where's that then? I asked Hilary a little bit more about this place and my heart began to sink because I realised I'd cancelled that audition.

'Damn it!'

But it was too late. I was heading to Mountview and I'd best get my head round it. Whilst a little disappointed in myself, I got ready for an autumn start and spent my time flicking through all the information that Mountview had sent me. Then one day I got a letter from them, informing me that the voice coach I'd worked with the day of my audition believed I had 'nodes' on my vocal cords that needed removing or I'd lose my voice within a year of starting my training. What? I read the letter a couple of times and later showed Mum at the wine bar. Even though I wasn't absolutely sure, I made an appointment at the surgery Mountview had recommended. Everything was all set for my operation, but I was uneasy about it. Something didn't sound right but what did I know? If they said that's what I needed, they must know what they're doing? A couple of days later, I was sitting at home when the house phone rang and when I picked it up the posh voice on the other end of the phone asked to speak to David Harewood.

'Yes, that's me,' I said.

'Ah, David. This is the registrar at the Royal Academy of Dramatic Art. I noticed you didn't attend your audition on Tuesday and I'm calling to see if everything is okay?'

I thought to myself, *Blimey, I cancelled that audition.* But I thought quickly on my feet and said:

'Yes, my mother was ill and I had to look after her. Sorry, I should have told you.'

He said, 'Not to worry. The reason I'm calling is that someone has dropped out of their audition tomorrow and I was wondering if you'd like to take their slot as you missed yours?'

I quickly surmised that they hadn't got my cancellation letter! So, I said:

'Yes, I'd love to take the place. What time should I be there?'

'Ten thirty a.m., David. Excellent. We'll see you there.'

I had that rush of energy again, the same one I had when I first thought about becoming an actor, and I quickly relearned my audition pieces and decided to learn a song. I turned to my parents' record collection and settled on the Bill Withers track

'Lovely Day', spending the afternoon learning the lyrics, picking up the needle of the record player and repeating each verse till I had it down. My old mate from school, Murphy, was with me and together we worked on the song and the speech. By the next day I had it all under my hat and was ready to give it my best. I travelled down to London in a T-shirt and jeans because it was scorching. I didn't have a care in the world and I thought to myself:

Just go and enjoy yourself.

And I did exactly that. This was a different kind of audition from the others, much more detailed and thorough. At the end of each section someone would walk in and read out a list of names and if your name wasn't called, you could stay for the next round. I kept getting through! I was there all day until eventually there was just me and one girl. I remember us both sitting in an empty classroom talking at the end of the day, thinking it was either her or me. After she'd gone in, it was my turn. I walked in to find the Principal of RADA, Oliver Neville, sitting there next to the same registrar that had called me about the audition. We spoke about the day and he asked me if I'd enjoyed it and then he said:

'You're actually very funny! I was watching you earlier and you managed to make me laugh with the things you were doing. Do you think you could make me laugh now?'

Talk about pressure! But I was a natural clown, I could pull something out of the bag, surely? I thought of something I did at the Christmas review night at school, a monologue I'd made up about a Rasta Santa Claus delivering his presents that had gone down a storm in front of my classmates, but doing it here I was dying a death. He hardly smiled at all, though the registrar was chuckling away. Let's just say I didn't really set the place alight. After a while I just stopped and told him that was all I had. He thanked me and before I knew it, I was heading back to Euston station kicking myself the whole way, thinking of ALL the really funny things I could have done instead. I was in a tailspin all the way home, convinced I'd blown my opportunity. I did my best to put it out of my head and forget all about it.

I didn't get any post for a week or so but one morning I had a dream that there was an important letter for me downstairs and as soon as I woke up, I went downstairs and peeked into the front room. There was a thin letter addressed to me. Now, going by my own experience, the thinner the letter, the more likely it was to be a 'No, thanks' because they wouldn't have sent through all the accompanying info on the school. Preparing myself for disappointment, I opened the letter and saw the words:

We are pleased to offer you a place on the acting course . . .

That's all I read. I couldn't believe it! I'd got into one of the best drama schools in the world! ME! I was over the moon. I told everybody. My family seemed happy and obviously everyone at the wine bar was beside themselves. Colin was telling all his posh customers I was heading to RADA. Hilary was telling all of her mates. Everybody was delighted for me and I was bursting with excitement myself. I cancelled my place at Mountview and, strangely enough, never heard another thing about the supposed 'nodes'. I was off to RADA! Now I had to work out where I was going to get the bloody money to pay for it.

I called up Mr Reader and told him the news. He was so proud and we both laughed, remembering how it all started, and considered the possibilities that lay ahead. Our talk soon moved on to how best to finance the course. It turned out I had to apply to the council for a discretionary grant, presenting my entrance to the prestigious RADA as evidence of talent. Hopefully, that would be enough for them to award me the cash. But there was a chance I would have to audition for my grant, and it was a notoriously tough audition.

As my appointment day drew near, my nerves were on edge. I arrived at a crusty old council building, all brown wood panelling and musty carpets. There were four kids there for the audition; one of the kids was with his mum, fussing over him, playing with his hair and telling him how fabulous he was.

'There's no one else like you, Simon. No one. It's your destiny, love! I've always said you're going to be a star.'

Simon seemed a bit embarrassed, but still looked like he had something about him, which is more than can be said for the bloke next to me. Something about this guy felt quite off, and he appeared to be playing with a couple of spoons. *Why has he got those spoons?* I wondered. Suddenly he started playing them, humming to himself, and I realised with shock that the spoons were part of his act. *He's here to play the fuckin' spoons, and the star kid over there's probably got the voice of an angel, and I'm here doing Shakespeare.* I actually started to get a bit nervous, feeling this was more of a talent show. Should I do something else? I started sifting through my options when the door opened and this bloke called my name.

'David Harewood?'

'Yep.'

Too late. I was heading in, stuck with the Shakespeare. I walked into the room and was hit with the smell of booze and fags. Back in those days you could smoke anywhere and this place stank of it.

'Sit yourself down, kid. Let me just get comfortable here. Right. So. You've got yourself into an acting school in London, have you?'

'Yes. The Royal Academy of Dramatic Art.'

'Right. And what do they do there then?'

'Well, they give you training in acting, like voice and, you know, sort of teach you about how best to work on characters and, basically, it really helps you get work.'

'Right.'

Silence as he read through my file.

'And you're gonna do some Shakespeare here now, are you?'

'I was thinking about it, yes.'

'Right.'

Silence.

'Okay. Well, off you go. In your own time.'

I stood up and did my usual audition – you know, the same one I did to get into bleedin' RADA! But he was stony-faced the whole way through and when I finished, after a short pause, he said:

'Can't stand that stuff.'

I said, 'Well, you have to know the play and the story.'

'Right.'

Silence.

'Well, thanks anyway, kid. Look, we 'er, we like to keep an open mind to everything and, you know, it's a busy year, we've got a lot of applicants. All I can say is that you should stay in touch and we'll be making our decision in due time. All right, kid?'

'Yeah, thanks.'

I was the only Black kid there that day and I could sense the privileged company I was in. As I was walking out the door angel-face Simon was walking in all smiles with his mum following behind. It sounded like they all knew each other. I briefly heard the sound of laughter between them before the door closed. I was alone with the spoon player as he waited for his own shot at fame and I had a sinking feeling. What if this doesn't work out? How am I going to get the money together to get to RADA if this doesn't break my way?

I was stuck in that anxious mindset for about three weeks wondering what was going to happen. I hadn't heard anything and it was getting me down. For the life of me I don't know how, but the story got into the local paper: 'Actor Plays Grant Drama!' basically saying how I'd won a place at RADA but was waiting for an answer from Birmingham Council as to whether I'd be able to afford to attend. Another week went by, and one afternoon I walked into the wine bar and saw Colin talking in hushed tones to a burly, roundish, bespectacled man who was leaning over the bar listening intently to Colin as he gave forth. I slipped into the kitchen to get ready for work and no sooner had I got my coat off than Colin popped his head in and told me to come out front. He wanted me to meet the guy he was talking to. I crossed over to shake his hand and spoke with him for about ten minutes. Colin had told him I'd been offered a place at RADA and that I was waiting for a grant from the council. He just wanted to talk to me about it and look me over. I didn't know who he was but after we'd spoken for a while, he said to Colin:

'All right, Col, I'll be off. I see what you mean. Seems a good 'un. I'll have a word and see what's happening. Thanks for the champagne. Love to the wife. All the best.'

And he was gone. Turns out he was the head of one of the biggest unions in the city and was something of a figure around town. I have no idea if he actually did anything, but a week later I was home with my dad when there was a knock at the door. When my father answered it, there was a bloke from the council standing outside. He came in and spoke to my dad about having to sign for my discretionary grant. I'd got it! My dad had to look it over carefully. I think he was worried about putting his name to it and committing to all that money. I remember him pausing before he signed it and looking at me and saying:

'Are you sure you're going to make any money out of this?'

'Yes, Dad.'

I just wanted him to sign it. I would have said anything and when he finally did, I knew I was on my way, and the biggest smile rolled across my face. I was going to RADA!

Everyone was delighted. Lui was so pleased and his family were absolutely thrilled. All of my friends were pumped about the news. Looking back, this is when I began to move away from my own family. Perhaps I was just a self-absorbed teenager, but with the family broken up now and all of us kids older, I let myself get swept up in the prospect of a new life and the bright lights of the business.

As the clock ticked down to my departure, I found myself eager to jump in and explore what was to come. It meant leaving behind everybody I'd grown up with and some people were a little concerned, not least my mum. I was moving down to London and there were many unknowns. But I felt confident because I'd been there before. I couldn't wait to go back.

On my final night working in the wine bar, a number of old faces passed through. It was a wonderful night of drinking and laughter. At one point, after we'd locked the doors, I found myself alone in the kitchen with Colin. I'd always seen him as this big man, but here he was fighting back tears. I was thanking him for all the years he had let me work there and everything he'd done. I proper thanked him, too, for helping me with the grant. I wasn't sure if that guy had done anything but I was still thankful. Colin told me that all his mates, all the 'Goodfellas', the wise guys, who over the years had heard me doing the speeches behind the bar all night, had decided they were going to pay the money themselves to get me to RADA if the grant hadn't worked out.

'David. We're all very proud of you. We would have done anything to see you succeed. Everyone said they would've chipped in. They all think the world of you. As do I.'

It was deep and meant a lot to me. We were both quite emotional for a minute, and it was really tough to walk out of there for the last time. I remember Colin specifically saying to me:

'Be careful down there. All that Black politics stuff.'

Something within me shifted, stirred, when he said it.

I didn't quite get why he said it at the time but in many ways Colin was very perceptive. He may have been salt-of-the-earth white Anglo-Saxon but he had a style and wisdom about him and an open, empathetic outlook. He knew right then and there I was an innocent, unprepared for the shark-infested waters of the wider world, not yet understanding the complexities that came along with what I was.

Black.

I'd neglected that part of my identity all these years. I was about to head off to play in the field of dreams, the world of study and literature and art and to make friendships that would last a lifetime, without yet understanding a fundamental part of my core identity. I'd assimilated to the point where I thought my colour really didn't matter. I had no knowledge of my Black self, no sense of the history and meaning, no sense of the story of my people and the rich culture from which I came. I think, fundamentally, this was one of the prime reasons why I fell so hard when I did. I'd built the house without setting the foundations.

A whole chapter of my life was now behind me and a new one lay sprawling ahead. I'd be leaving Birmingham and living the student life. I was single now, and eager to explore the nocturnal hours with an eye for adventure. I didn't know much about the business side of acting, and I was sure there'd be others more gifted than I was, but I was going in full confidence, perhaps born of ignorance. I just wanted to immerse myself in the teaching, learn and see what would become of it. I started out full of beans, but somewhere along the line this buoyant young man became the lost soul that turned up at Whittington Hospital deluded and hallucinating. Something happened, something went seriously wrong and I spiralled out of control. We're getting closer to that storm, but for now it's time for training and learning at the Royal Academy. The universe had provided and I was headed for RADA.

Chapter Seven

The Building That Will Change
My Life Forever

It's an unassuming place. I'm sure a lot of people walk right past it and don't even know it's there. Although it's much changed now, back then I felt like I was walking in the footsteps of history. There are many named actors who have studied at RADA. It's known and respected around the world. Not everybody who goes there will automatically be a success, but it bestows a mark of recognition, much like Oxford or Cambridge, or Juilliard. Having the name behind you can be enough of a platform to launch a young actor.

I remember my first day, feeling a little daunted and navigating my way to the first group meeting. We checked each other out, polite and respectful, as we shared the space throughout the day. At one point all the new students were sitting in a circle as Oliver Neville, the principal, held court and asked the group what sort of writers and plays we most admired. I sat there for about ten minutes while names I'd never heard of rolled off tongues as if they were familiar friends: Chekhov, Brecht, Johnson and Pinter. For a moment I felt like an idiot. I thought to myself:

Maybe I don't belong here?

I was aware I hadn't said anything and when finally Oliver asked me my thoughts, I just decided honesty was the best policy.

'I've never heard of these people! I've probably read two plays in my life but I'm really looking forward to getting to know more about all this.'

Oliver smiled. I understood that I didn't know as much as some of the others in the group, but I'd got into the place, so I figured I must have something to offer. I could always learn and expand my understanding – after all, that's what I was there for. It was a wonderful grounding in the basics of the art. Teaching centred around the voice and the body. We were split into different groups for our voice classes and I landed with the most eccentric and wonderful voice coach in Jeffrey Connor. His descriptive and passionate teaching had us all in fits of laughter. We'd meet up in various group classes for movement, acting and other physical work. Dotted around the weekly calendar would be text study, where you'd be given pieces to work on and study. There'd also be the stage-fighting classes, something I particularly loved because I enjoyed learning the skills of combat and battling with the various weapons we had at our disposal. When the doors to the sword cabinet were opened, I was like a kid in a sweetshop. All I could think about was *Spartacus* and *The Three Musketeers*! Silly, I know, but I'd seen so many sword fights in movies as a kid that every time the cupboard opened I was transported to a totally different world.

We were a very different group from what one might have expected a typical RADA year to look like. Our principal, Oliver, said he wanted to move away from the standard Royal Academy type and allow room for individuality, so there were more working-class kids in my year. For the first time I wasn't the only Black person in the room. We all bonded pretty quickly, the chemistry working very well. Some had already been to university, others had taken a different route, but we were all keen to be there. I think between us we were aware that we were something of a 'new broom'. It was in the pub just across the road, The Marlborough Arms, where the friendships solidified. After a long day of study, a sizable group began to make the place a home from home and as the beer and whisky flowed, we opened up to each other and created lasting friendships and strong bonds.

Finding somewhere to live was a bit of a challenge and I think I spent more than a couple of nights sleeping on various sofas and floors, but it didn't seem to matter. I'd be up bright-eyed the next day, if somewhat hungover, and rush back eager for more teaching. As a first-year student at RADA, you're something of a newbie and you look up to the years above. They have enviable confidence because they're familiar with the building and more secure in themselves. They've already been through the rigours of the first year and can't help but cast an eye over the newcomers. Final year students are busy performing plays and rehearsing and getting ready for the real world outside. They had little time for us, but it was amazing to watch them in their shows. They seemed so mature. It was hard to picture ourselves in the same position even though we'd be there in no time at all. For now, we marvelled at their acting and regarded them as the real deal, on the brink of conquering the world and becoming young superstars.

By term's mid-point, a group of us were fast friends. I had become particularly close to Danny, Jez, Nick and Jane. Somehow, Danny managed to find us a house to move into together in Hendon, North London. It was a wonderful time! If we weren't drinking in the pub, we were sitting next to each other in class, studying or just plain laughing our asses off at home, we were pretty inseparable. But there were changes happening, too. I was paying attention in my voice classes and my speech was beginning to change. I'd arrived at RADA with a pretty solid Brummie accent, but as I grew to love the vowel sounds contained in classic texts my pronunciation shifted. Some say that by losing your accent, you dilute your authenticity. There are many who choose not to lose this part of their identity, but I didn't want to spend my life playing Brummies. I purposefully ironed out my accent in order to be able to adapt. I've always enjoyed doing different accents and I saw no downside in having a more neutral sound, but this adaptability didn't always work in my favour. Over the years some have accused me of selling out, with claims that having good diction was almost equivalent to being a 'coconut': Black on the outside but all white on the inside. This was yet another arrow that would lead to my unravelling as I tried to carve out an identity that gave me confidence and kept me in work. Criticism coming from so many directions caused confusion in my young mind. Before my fall, though, I was enjoying my voice classes and enjoying being able to create sounds with my voice that I hadn't thought imaginable.

I hadn't really paid attention to my studies in the past, but here at drama school I began to appreciate the wonder of the literary classics, especially all the visual images contained in the writing. It was a real revelation to me, a working-class boy from Birmingham falling in love with the words of eighteenth-century poets. I wondered what it would be like to be able to write like that and construct a lasting piece that encapsulated in beautiful verse how it felt to be in love with another person. I was finding a growing appreciation of the words I was getting to work with every day.

Before I knew it, we only had a couple of weeks to go before the end of our first year. We were told what plays we would be performing in the following year and we all instantly started guessing what the casting would be. We were to be split into two groups. One group would perform *King Lear* and the other would be doing *Romeo and Juliet*. Guesses were made as to who would be playing what roles. I had half an idea I might play Tybalt in *Romeo and Juliet* as it was a role Hugh Quarshie, one of the country's premier Black actors, had played at the Royal Shakespeare Company that year. He had made quite a stir with his performance and something told me they might go in a similar direction, but I kept it to myself. At drama school you don't necessarily get the roles you want, more the roles you need.

As we were about to return to our homes for the summer break, we were encouraged to keep up our vocal work and pay attention to what we'd learned over our first term. I headed back to Birmingham sounding like Jeeves and Wooster, much to the surprise of my mother. I think she was pretty alarmed and gave me the side eye whenever I pronounced the word 'bath' as 'barth'. It was all too much for her. I explained that the affected way I was speaking was a result of the teaching, but I think she worried about these subtle changes because her boy was morphing into something else. I popped up to the wine bar to see the old team. Not much had changed there and I think I even worked a couple of nights. It was good to see everyone and fill them in on what I was spending my days doing. I sat with Lui and chatted about London. He was doing well himself and had landed a promising sales job. He'd be good at that: he could sell coals to Newcastle. He was great company and funny and we laughed a lot.

The summer went by quickly, but even so, I couldn't wait to get back to London and the new life I'd created for myself amongst a talented and brilliant set of new friends. I'd fallen in love with London, the pace of it, the edge of it, wandering into grimy Soho after a late night and sitting outside Bar Italia. There was something so exciting about it all. Sitting on the train heading back to my studies, my mind drifted to the plays we'd be doing that term and as we pulled into London Euston, I decided to walk down to RADA and pop my head in the door to see if the plays had been cast. There was still a week or two before the start of term and I was early into the building, but as I walked through the front doors I passed one of the teachers and he looked at me and said:

'Congratulations, David!'

I asked him what he meant and he told me to go and look at the cast list pinned on the wall of a noticeboard on the second level. I walked up and glanced at the list and to my shock I saw:

King Lear – David Harewood

Fuck! My knees buckled. *Me? Play King Lear? Jesus Christ.* I wandered out of the building in something of a daze, with a strange sense of fear and excitement. I walked straight down to the bookshop on the corner, bought a copy of the play and started reading. This was the play that had blown me away as a young kid all those years ago and here I was going to be the central character, the king who goes mad. It's an astonishing piece of imagination and remains my favourite Shakespeare play, with its monumental character arcs that collide in spectacular fashion. I had a wonderful time exploring the themes of the play and was fortunate to have the most amazing director in Stephen

Dartnell. He really took time to guide me through the text and gave me an incredibly useful note for reading scripts. He took me aside one evening after a rehearsal and casually asked me if I smoked weed?

'Erm . . . occasionally . . .'

He said, 'Well, if you do, when you're at home studying the play, don't learn your lines, stare at the page. Just stare across the text and after a while you'll see images buried in there. Take time to see the images.'

I did. It is indeed a great way to study a play. But it must be said that smoking weed can also contribute to developing psychosis. At this point in time, though, I didn't even know what psychosis was. I was living and breathing acting and acting alone, and especially my new role as King Lear.

Lear gives away all his power to two of his daughters who cast him out. That they are his own children only adds to the pain:

'Reason not the need,' cries the King when his child questions why he needs his entourage, why he needs anything. His stress and confusion increase and he finds himself wandering the heath and railing at the storm. His new life is incompatible with what he has known before, the majesty and pomp; the jarring new reality that confronts him is enough to break him and upon seeing a poor naked soul wandering out in the open, he finally sees how as King he took little notice of the poor and homeless in his kingdom. In response, he proceeds to strip himself naked in solidarity with the real people in his former kingdom and in doing so loses his grip on reality. It's the most wonderful character arc and I thoroughly enjoyed my journey into the part.

Each day I had a deeper understanding and it was the first time that I'd really taken myself seriously as an actor. Prior to playing Lear, I don't think I'd really appreciated how much I loved acting and that I might actually have a knack for it. As the weeks passed by I found myself growing into the role and maturing with each day. Just before a run-through one afternoon, Stephen took me aside and told me not to be afraid of the emotion in the play.

'Allow yourself to be vulnerable,' he said.

I've always enjoyed getting a good note from a director and this was no different. Something in me opened up the moment we started the run-through and I felt the passion and emotion straight away. It's never good to get too caught up in the emotion of a piece, but sometimes in a play, when everything comes together, there seems to be no difference between you and the character you're playing. I found so many different colours to play in that run, particularly during the madness scenes. It was like I'd been freed from all restraint as I pushed myself to take risks and do things I'd hadn't dared to in rehearsals.

I went on to play some wonderfully interesting characters for the rest of my time at RADA. I was enjoying my acting and performing in comedies, dramas and classics. It seemed as though I had found my groove. Nobody ever mentioned my colour, and I played a range of roles in which there didn't appear to be any issue with what I looked like.

As wonderful as my time at RADA was, the experience gave me a false sense of the real world. Before I knew it, we were in the final stretch of our degree, when agents were beginning to show an interest in some of the students as we performed our last shows. The wild and crazy nights in Hendon were over, Danny and Jane moved on while me, Nick and Jez moved into a flat in Crouch End, sharing the space with a friend of Jez who was a sound engineer. It was a cool little spot, I was always working so it served me well and it was great to still be in touch with Nick and Jez. I got lucky and was immediately snapped up by a very reputable agent, Pat Marmont. Pat was an old-school dame of the business who took me on with a view to continuing my classical journey and providing me with a thorough grounding in professional theatre. There still weren't many Black actors working regularly on British television and there really wasn't anybody of my own generation I could look to emulate. I trusted Pat's guidance and agreed to sign with her. I was keen for the journey ahead and her vision seemed exciting.

A few weeks before the end of my final term, Pat introduced me to Alby James, artistic director of one of Britain's premier Black theatre groups, Temba Theatre Company. I remember our first meeting, the audition, the smile on his face. I was cast as Romeo in his brand-new, ambitious production of *Romeo and Juliet*, set to start production in Manchester and tour for eight weeks before returning to London at the Young Vic. I was excited about taking it on. It was a pretty high-profile gig. Alby had positioned the production as something of a shot across the bows of the establishment, proving that Black actors could perform the classics with equal aplomb and fill theatres just the same as white companies could. I was all for that. There was a lot of pre-press, photo shoots and interviews, but I hadn't imagined that the interviews would leave me feeling so exposed. I hadn't considered some of the questions that might be put to me:

'Shakespeare didn't write the part for a Black actor; do you think it's stretching the imagination to have a Black Romeo?'

What?

I was unsure of myself and found it difficult to navigate many of the questions. I was spending more time justifying why I was cast than discussing the merits of the production. I really wasn't comfortable in the role. There was something about the production that didn't inspire me and I felt ineffective. Unlike the parts I'd played at RADA, where I'd loved the process, suddenly I wasn't quite as settled. After playing so long with close colleagues at drama school, the lack of familiar faces around me was destabilising. My friend Joe Dixon was in the production, however, and was an excellent Mercutio. Without some light moments with Joe, I probably would have struggled sooner.

I wasn't enjoying myself on stage and that was a first. No matter how hard I tried, I couldn't get myself going in the role. The constant touring and weekly moves made it a tough shift. The reviews were generally okay, but I noticed that the production was always referred to as a 'Black' production, and I was always a 'Black' actor. At RADA I'd just been an actor. Now my colour was the defining factor in reviews and articles.

Up to this point I hadn't developed an understanding of the core part of my identity that was most obvious to others, my Blackness. Growing up, there had been little opportunity to explore Black culture and be around people of colour. I understood Black culture through the records and lyrics heard in my mum and dad's collection, as well as understanding the themes of American funk and soul, but I hadn't managed to apply it all on a deeper level to myself. Assimilation meant looking out and not looking in. It was by looking out that I'd ended up following my dreams and becoming an actor, but I probably decided to do my first professional job in Black theatre driven by a need to belong.

Being young and eager, I often read reviews. I'm not sure what I was expecting but I suppose I was looking for a little love and some acknowledgement. The more I read, however, the more I understood that white culture, the white space, was dismissing me and robbing me of any individuality and personality. After a while I stopped reading notices, because it appeared to be a competition to see who could write the most damning piece.

I can remember once playing Othello out of town at the Swan Theatre in Worcester and I got the worst review I've ever had in my life. It was so personal and rude that my director called up the local paper asking for an explanation. She was told that the regular critic didn't actually write the piece. Instead, it had been written by a young staffer. They acknowledged that the review fell well below acceptable standards, but it was too late to do anything about it. I felt I had to toughen up and not let critical responses upset me, but that was easier said than done. When the production finally came into London, where I thought minds might be a little more open, I realised I was sorely mistaken. The review I read the morning after the first night commented that I:

'Looked more like Mike Tyson than Romeo.'

That was one of the last reviews I read before my breakdown. I promised myself never to read another. I was finished with the white space. After years of rejection, I simply found it too painful. When the production ended I was relieved, but in retrospect, my problems were only just beginning. Within a year, I would find myself locked on a psychiatric ward. As I write this, I see the countdown clock starting to tick down; everything that happens from here on in will take me a step closer to losing my mind.

If I was in London, I was home and if I was at home, I was probably smoking weed. With everything that was going on in my life – a perceived failure (Romeo), all the racial questions swirling around within me – I needed some relief. I had a dawning awareness of that little piece of me that had broken off the moment I'd first been racially abused:

Little Black bastard.

I could appreciate that experience in a different way: realising that my otherness had no value in the white space. I felt I needed to make adjustments to my thinking, downgrading what would be achievable for me, clipping my wings, letting go of my dreams. It was the end of other things too, Nick and Jez had decided they were moving out and moving on. After living together for two years of college, the time had come to go our separate ways. For me, that's when I realised a chapter in my life had come to a close. I wasn't a young student anymore, I was a working actor and I needed somewhere to live. Luckily for me, Jez's friend found a place in Islington, a really nice two bedroom flat, and on the spot we decided we'd move in together. Neither of us were there much, he kept odd hours as a sound engineer, coming in in the middle of the night and crashing out just before the sun came up. Maybe not having my familiar friends around all the time increased my sense of solitude. I'd come home from a gig to an empty flat and just start smoking and drinking, numbing the discomfort I was feeling from the world outside. I would lose my mind in this apartment, the clock was already ticking though I was oblivious to it. I carried on working and did a couple of small TV jobs but it was the next theatre gig that tipped me over the edge. It broke me and pinpoints the time everything went badly wrong. Alby had asked me to lead another show.

In the early 1990s there was a push to form a Black section of the official British Labour Party and although it was eventually defeated, it signalled the growing confidence and presence of an emerging Black British identity. This play attempted to wrap up all the issues about 'Black sections' in a light-hearted play. On reading it seemed like an interesting piece, but something deep down in me wasn't convinced. I paused my decision but Alby was very persuasive, saying we could work on things during rehearsal:

'I think you should do it,' I remember him saying.

I should never have done it. It was a disaster. I don't want to go into all of the details, but it fell apart very quickly. After a short run, we took the play on a tour. There was someone in the company I had a particularly difficult time with because they were playing a lot of psychological games with me and getting uncomfortably close. I'd not experienced this before, and I didn't quite know how to handle it. Relationships became very fraught in the company as the play began to disintegrate, and on stage it was pretty much every man for himself.

My character ended up being the punchline to every bad gag and I had the sense that the audience was laughing at me, personally. My insecurities started playing up and going on stage became difficult. For the first time ever, I was beginning to lose my nerve. It felt as if the 'Black space' was rejecting me too. The bullying and game-playing I suffered went from bad to worse and uncomfortably close got uncomfortably closer. I guess you could say, it was my very own 'Me Too' moment.

After that, things deteriorated. I identify this moment as the straw that broke the camel's back. I totally withdrew. There were still eight or nine weeks left on the tour so there was no way I could get out of my situation. I'd have to face this person every night whilst being laughed at by a majority Black audience.

In the theatre, as actors, we are given a thirty-minute warning call to let everybody know it's countdown to the start of the show. It's followed by a fifteen, a five, and then a beginners' call when all actors and crew involved in the first scene of the play are to take their places ready for lights up. For many actors it's almost a ritual. I usually loved getting to the theatre at least an hour before the half (thirty-minutes call). Just to chill and focus I'd do a physical and a vocal warm-up, get my costume on and use the thirty minutes to prepare psychologically. That was my routine, but on this play I'd arrive an hour early but instead of chilling, just to get through the night, I'd head straight to the front-of-house bar and drink till the five! Then I'd rush back-stage, quickly get changed, do the show, go home and drink some more. Then I'd wake up and repeat. It was a one-off, but it was a very difficult gig for me and caused an enormous amount of harm to my mental health. I actually performed the last night in my own clothes so after the curtain call, I just walked off stage, picked up my bag and fucked off.

The switch was flipped. I was probably already starting to spin a little by now, my mind slipping away without my noticing it. I returned to London and was smoking weed as usual. I was so keen to put that bad experience behind me that I was probably especially high spirited, happy to be free of all the shit. But I wouldn't be home for long. I got a wonderful offer to head up to the Derby Playhouse and play Sloane in Joe Orton's *Entertaining Mr Sloane*, a fabulous play that caused a scandal in its original production for its dark humour and lewd language. It was just what I needed, to be doing some comedy and putting all the politics behind me.

I had the pleasure of working with a cast of real pros. We put a really dark but very funny production together. Sloane is a great part. Devious, cunning and utterly shameless, he works his way through the play taking advantage of everyone he can until finally he's trapped in a web he can't escape. Along the way, though, Sloane creates havoc, killing a granddad and shagging both a husband and the wife! I had a riot on stage. These actors I was working with were so old-school fantastic, surfing a laugh from the audience and milking comedy moments. It was great to be playing with them and the show was a hit all round. I can remember backstage, though, that things weren't all well. In the actors' bar I sensed people weren't sure of me. Some thought I was arrogant. Perhaps it's because the part was very much out there and maybe people thought that was what I was really like. Either way, I could feel the backstage crew giving me a wide berth. I got my head down and enjoyed the play.

Productions are full of all different types of personalities. If you're lucky, you won't have any off-beam actors but there are no guarantees. Maybe I was the off-beam one this time? Considering how my mental health was at that point, they were probably right. I hadn't read any reviews but I heard they were great. Finally, I couldn't resist taking a peek. They were nice! Generally five star and it gave me a bit of a buzz, but then I came across a letter in a local Black newspaper where someone had seen the play and had written that it was a disgusting piece and that I should be ashamed of myself for appearing in it. It was a bit of a shock, but then next night, during a very explicit monologue Sloane gives at the beginning of the second act, I noticed a bit of movement in the audience. As I continued with the piece I saw that it was a young Black couple walking out. I pushed on, thinking it was a little weird, but the next night at the same place, during this rather dark tale Sloane gives, again a couple of Black people walked out. It was only ever Black members of the audience that walked out, and they did it around the same part of the play. It happened randomly throughout the whole run and it really began to get under my skin. It seemed like another rejection from the Black space and I found myself getting angry. I started reacting to these walkouts, badly, almost playing with those walking out and incorporating it into my performance.

One particular night I felt on fire. I reckon the psychosis was already kicking in because it seemed as though I was flying and full of energy. Afterwards the stage manager caught me on my way to the bar and told me that I'd taken eight minutes off the runtime of the play! He said when disarming and killing the old man with his cane, instead of dropping it as I had done on previous nights, I'd flicked it over the top of the set and it had disappeared and couldn't be found. He had to replace it the next night. Going home at night and thinking about why those audience members walked out, I guessed that the subject matter of the play, particularly the homosexual content, was a little too much for their sensibilities. Maybe their discomfort was amplified because I was Black. My colour again! I'd never thought about it so much. Every day, I was running comprehensive Q&As in my head, questioning myself about my own authenticity. *If Black audiences are rejecting me, maybe I don't belong here?* I became unsure of myself again. I had questions about who and what I was.

I'd thought I could play *anyone.* I was in such a creative space at RADA, and colour wasn't mentioned, so I felt anything was possible. But since I'd come out of drama school, I'd found it wasn't true. Now all I thought about was the complexities of race and my own ideas of what it meant. I was putting together a whole new understanding, slowly readjusting my sails in unfamiliar, choppy waters. I was no longer the fun-loving life of the party I had once been and I remember struggling socially, retreating into my own world once outside the theatre.

When the run was finished, I came back to London and started my usual routine of smoking and staying up late at night. It was good to be home, but I was in a weird mental state. I must have entered the manic period of the psychosis, when my thoughts began racing. This was compounded because I was overstimulating my mind with alcohol and weed. Throughout I was still auditioning, meeting casting agents and going up for

TV gigs. My routine seemed ordinary but there was something amiss. I had an audition in town for a TV gig one day and I set off for Windmill Street in London's West End. I had walked past Windmill Street every other day as a student and knew exactly where it was. But when I got off the Tube, all the noise and shapes and colours confused me. I became lost in a maze of life. I knew I was there for an audition but I didn't know where I was. I found a phone box and called my agent:

'What was that address again?'

Still couldn't find it. Finally, after what seemed like thirty or forty minutes, I arrived at the audition. I was three hours late. I don't remember what the gig was but the casting agent was a great lady by the name of Janey Fothergill. She picked up that I wasn't well and sat with me talking till she could work out what was best to do. I think she called my agent, who called Nick and Jez, and they drove into town to pick me up and take me home. Apparently I was like a child when leaving the audition with them. My mind was breaking down.

The delusions were now crashing into reality, but somehow I just kept going. The psychosis firmly taking a grip, I was lost in a continual cycle of auditioning, reading books and comics, and cutting out pictures in magazines and pinning them on my clothing. Although I hadn't stopped working since I'd left drama school, each of my big theatre experiences had been bruising affairs, particularly the second. Pottering about my flat, I was just happy to be home in a familiar environment and listening to music. I simply lost track of things. It was an oddly creative time. I created a separate personality: Secret Agent Man! I could go ANYWHERE, do ANYTHING. As Secret Agent Man I could literally be ANYONE. I sort of mentally wanted to break out of the box I'd found myself in:

Just a Black actor.

Just Black.

Black.

Not Black enough.

I was overthinking things. I would go for long walks around London, merely on a whim. I'd be gone for hours. Dr Erin Turner, the lead psychiatrist in *Psychosis and Me*, asked me to give her an example of some of the things I did on these walks. I told her of a time I was out walking really early one morning and across the road walking towards me was this rough-looking white dude walking this huge Doberman Pinscher and it appeared to be looking right at me. I crossed the road, looking straight at the dog, and asked the guy:

'What's your dog's name, bruv?'

He said, 'Jebb.'

I fixed the dog with a stare, leaned into its face and very, very firmly in a raised voice called its name:

'JEBB.'

The fucking dog was whelping and crying, rolling around on its back and freaking the fuck out!

'What you done to my dog?'

Dr Turner told me that some dogs do pick up on certain mental health conditions; I bet cats do too! But I'll never forget that moment. I must admit, the energy I was feeling around this time was really exciting. I knew I was experiencing something, but I thought if I could control it, I could let my imagination fly and create something very special. Maybe it would be a unique type of theatrical experience that I'd write and direct myself. I'd cast all my friends, create a company of actors and produce revolutionary work. I'd have to build a new type of theatre with rails on the ceiling so we could play scenes up there and . . . and . . .

and . . . and . . . I was spinning. Right about now Dr Turner would have been strongly suggesting I head to early intervention, go to see a professional, because I was already in the grip of a serious mental health crisis. With due care I could have avoided the next, and most difficult, chapter of my life.

It's good to know that I can now write that next chapter from a place of strength. If there's one thing I've learned looking back, it's how resilient I am. I find it astonishing that I was able to come through a psychotic breakdown and snap right back into acting. Making the documentary and writing this book have helped me to understand the truth about my psychotic experience. This journey has helped me find a missing piece to the puzzle I've been putting together for the last thirty or forty years.

Perhaps because I'm a creative person my psychotic episode was particularly florid and dramatic, but I see the roots of it as being a gradual build-up of stress and questions of identity around my race. One night I was fast asleep when my flatmate nudged me on the shoulder:

'Dave? Dave?'

'Yeah.'

'You awake?'

'Yeah, yeah.'

'Erm . . . Where's the hash? That block we were smoking last night?'

I lay there thinking for a second, trying to put my day together.

'The hash?' I thought for a second longer, then it hit me. I'd got up that morning and dressed all smart, and for some reason I'd walked to Buckingham Palace and stuffed this big chunk of hashish in a gap between two slabs of pavement! I'd then started dancing. Within minutes I was swarmed by police cars and cops jumped out. I was totally calm and in my best RADA voice explained that I was an actor and I was just doing a bit of research for a role. I gave them all my details freely, talked about playing Romeo and came across completely authentically. They called RADA, my name checked out, and they asked me to let them know next time I wanted to 'rehearse' by the palace. I took that as a win and made my way home but I'd completely forgotten about the lump of hash I buried in between the slabs outside the palace. My flatmate looked at me like WTF?

I said:

'I know exactly where it is. I pushed it into the dirt really deep. I bet it's still there.'

He looked at me again and after a pause I said:

'Let's go get it!'

We jumped in the car and drove straight to Buckingham Palace. I was used to coming around very quickly now and I was chatting and laughing as we drove through the night towards the hash. I knew where it was; we slowly drove around to the front of the palace and I jumped out. I walked over to where I'd buried the stash. It didn't take me long. There, between two slabs of concrete outside Buckingham Palace, was our lump of hash! I dug it out, sprinted back to the car, drove home and got stoned.

Days later I remember waking at two in the afternoon, sweating, hot and gasping for breath. It felt like my skin was on fire, everything I touched seemed to burn me, but strangely, only things the colour of blue were cold. I grabbed a blue T-shirt and buried my head and hands in it. It felt like ice, so refreshing. I curled up in a ball on the floor, hugging the shirt, and went back to sleep. Then I was up again and out of the house, walking up the middle of the street in the dead of night, and I got this notion out of nowhere to get into the next car that stopped near me.

When a car pulled up at a set of traffic lights, I opened the door of the car and jumped in. The guy driving freaked out! I'm not surprised, he must have been terrified. But what would have happened if he wasn't? What if there'd have been others in the car? I was out of control, in and out of consciousness and lucidity.

I spent the nights walking through town. One time, I bumped into my old mate Clive Owen. We'd been at RADA at the same time and we'd always got along well and here in the midst of my mental breakdown I was standing in front of him. I kept telling him:

'I'm a genius! I'm a genius!'

We talked for a short while and I walked off. I saw him years later and we spoke about it. I told him that I'd been having a breakdown and that shortly after meeting him I'd been sectioned. I remember him saying something really odd. He said I was roller-skating. He was absolutely convinced that I was roller-skating. I don't own a pair of roller-skates and can't roller-skate! But he was absolutely sure of it.

A few nights after that I sat in front of the mirror smoking weed and drinking and I convinced myself that my reflection was actually the real me and because I'd found myself out, it was time for us to switch places and continue each other's lives. It was a deep night. Hallucinating is a common feature of psychosis. Believing that the clouds are sending you messages or that you can control the weather, you become convinced that somehow you have supernatural powers and are receiving messages from different realms. Every time you think you witness genuine 'communication' with the other world, it feels extraordinary.

I was in my flat bugging out one day, drawing pictures and writing lots of notes, when suddenly I thought of Danny. For some reason I knew I would see him. I got up and walked out of my house. No sooner had I closed the door and turned up the street than I saw Danny walking in the opposite direction! By now, it must have been the case that my old friends were concerned and had decided to keep an eye on me. I was hallucinating and had probably already seen him, which is why he was on my mind, but still, seeing him in the street that day felt slightly unnerving. Danny tells me I had this odd look on my face as he approached me, I don't really remember what we did but he spent some time with me before I crashed out. When I woke up later, I heard voices coming from another room so I got up to see where they were coming from. As I walked into the living room I saw Danny, Nick and Jez. It felt odd waking up to see them all in one place again. Really lovely but, fuck! The gang's back together! I was so excited to see them that I launched straight into another passionate stream of consciousness of ideas, but they could sense that something wasn't right. They tried to talk to me about maybe seeing someone at a hospital, just to check things out. I wasn't interested. I accepted that I wasn't feeling 100 per cent but I was wary of seeing a doctor. I brushed them off and promised them I was fine. I carried on pushing deeper into the energy.

I went out walking again, obsessed with the idea that I was invisible and that I was disappearing. The only way I could find safety was to become an invisible man. It actually makes some sense when I think about that now. I had come to the conclusion that I was invisible because as I walked around the West End, looking at the billboards and posters and advertisements, I realised there wasn't a single Black image to be seen. I couldn't see myself anywhere. It's different now, of course, with more inclusive imagery in campaigns, but this was the early '90s. There was a growing fear that I'd completely misjudged my chosen field. *How the hell am I going to succeed if I don't exist?*

The moments between lucidity and psychosis were getting shorter. The hallucinations intensified and bright colours became vividly alive and appeared to be communicating with me. Every shape in the room dazzled me with perfection while the true chaotic randomness of life revealed its beauty to me. I sat for hours, rigid, still, staring forwards.

My mind was slipping away. My old RADA flatmate Jane appeared one day with Danny. It's only now I realise that all my old friends had come to see to because they feared I was not well and wanted to help in some way, but I kept brushing off their concerns about my state of mind, kept making light of it. They took me for a walk up by Regent's Park Zoo. I must have been pretty out of it but, as we were sitting together on a park bench, we over-heard a mother and son talking in the most ridiculously funny way to each other. All three of us looked at each other and immediately started laughing. I really remember that, it was the first time that day that I felt that I was normal again, that I was just out in the park with my old friends Danny and Jane enjoying life. But very quickly I lost focus and everything drifted back into noise. We walked back to the flat and there, again, were Nick and Jez.

My friends were now very concerned. Eventually they got through to me that my behaviour was deteriorating and that I should go with them to see a doctor. I knew I wasn't well because I would collapse with exhaustion and sleep for hours. When I'd wake up they'd have to start the conversation again. I was deeply suspicious of speaking to someone about what was going on inside my mind, how the fuck would they know anything? I'm not crazy, I'm not. I'm fine. It took a while to get me to actually go, I resisted, but eventually I found myself in front of a duty psychiatrist. I was extremely distrustful throughout the interview. I guess

I was a little combative too, challenging him on different concepts of what was real and what wasn't. For some reason I had a little plastic green man from some game I had at home in my pocket and I subtly put it on his desk. After a short while I said to him:

'What would you say if I told you I can see a little green man in this room right now?'

'A little green man?'

'Yes.'

He rolled his eyes. I could see my little green man clear as day on the desk. So I told him not to think so literally and take a look. We got into it a little. I knew I was flying a bit but the mere fact that he wouldn't even look for the little green man really bugged me. After a pretty strong back and forth I pointed to my little green man that had been on his desk for the last fifteen minutes.

'There it is!'

'That's ridiculous,' he said.

'It's not ridiculous. It's a little green man!'

I must admit, I do find it funny that thirty-odd years later, as a result of playing my current character in the American television series *Supergirl*, the Martian Manhunter, who just happens to be green, I still have a little green man on my desk as I write this!

I walked out of the psychiatrist's office after the assessment and sat with my friends. It wasn't long before he approached with a bottle of pills.

'Take three of these a day and try to get some sleep.'

One of my friends asked if I was okay and the psychiatrist turned and said, 'He just thinks he's Lenny Henry.'

I heard that and I was really pissed off. All respect to Lenny but I didn't like the lazy, casual association and I was immediately dubious of this guy; all of us were. When he walked off, we all stood for a moment in common understanding and I threw the bottle of pills in the bin. I was definitely not well, and this assessment could have been a crucial opportunity for me to pull out of my psychotic spiral, but it hadn't gone well and I was going home alone again.

I was about to have the most extraordinary night of my entire psychotic experience that would end up with me being arrested and locked in a cell somewhere in London, unable to remember my name. I was lying in bed sleeping when I heard what I thought was a big gust of wind and a voice out of nowhere whispered in my ear:

'W-W-WAKE UP!'

I sat bolt upright in bed, thinking, *What the fuck was that?*

This voice was inside my head?

'Don't be afraid. I know this seems very unusual, but you need to get up right now.'

It was an American voice, lyrical and familiar, and he told me he couldn't tell me who he was just yet as I wasn't ready. I was to get up, get dressed and walk to Camden Town to a clothes shop. I was to walk into the clothes shop, head to the back and then into the first changing room and there, in the room, a brand-new suit would be hanging up. He said I was to put the suit on and the moment I turned around and walked out of the changing room, it would be a completely different day and time but I would have taken part in a huge spiritual operation that would change the lives of millions of people! I was sitting in my bedroom listening to some strange unearthly entity talking to me, instructing me to get ready for a supernatural task. I got up and got ready, all the while in conversation with the voice in my head, ironed a pair of trousers and a shirt, slipped into a pair of shoes and was ready for my little adventure.

'I think you're ready to know who I am, David. Before we leave this house I must know that you believe in me, therefore I think it best I reveal myself to you now.'

'Okay.'

'You've had me in your heart for many years now, I've felt your love and understanding, and we are all blessed to be together again. David, my name is Martin Luther King.'

I burst into tears! *Oh my God. Me! You? How? Martin?* I sat there in my bedroom sobbing; this was the most amazing thing to ever happen to me. My guiding star was speaking to me. He went on to explain that when I played him as a kid in school, I had taken him into my heart where he had lived as a spirit for years. Now, tonight, I was one of a group of people around the world that he had 'activated' from heaven in order to complete a small task that would close the spiritual gap between good and evil. This. Was. Huge. It took me a few minutes to consider the scope of this task and all the while Martin Luther King was speaking to me in this booming voice echoing around my head. It was truly the most extraordinary thing I've ever experienced and because this voice seemed totally independent of me, it was incredibly believable. I was in the service of the spirit world, on a task to close the gap between good and evil, being spurred on by the voice of Martin Luther King. I opened the front door and stepped out into the warm London night. I was bound for a clothes shop in Camden to change the world, what could possibly go wrong?

Me at age five in primary school.

Me, centre right, with my sister Sandra and brothers Roger and Paul 1969-70.

Sports day, aged five. Winner!

Me aged five in front of my Dad's Ford Zephyr. We had a car while many neighbours didn't, so we always felt getting in it was a special occasion. This was Oldknow Road, the people across the road were a little envious! See them peering at us.

My mum and dad in 1972.

Some of my first headshots, taken in 1985.

Me and my mate Lui. He'd come to watch me perform *Othello*.

Patient's Name: A/E No.:

Not eating
No sleeping
Talking INAPPROPRIATE
today.night

OK Aggressive
       Grinning
       INAPPROPRIATE
   Fixed eye

IAP ① → ? HYPOMANIC
       ② ? DRUGS INDUCED

REFER PSYCHE   MY NEW CAPTAIN

---

888 8311 / 800 012, St Annes   307 3071
St. Lukes.   636 8333 Middx Dr Rifkind

15 Attempt to talk to him in a room on his
own (6 policemen outside door) — he only
shouted about "saving the boy" - "leave me
alone. don't touch me". And came towards
me to push me away.
Shouting at top of voice.

6 policemen + 1 male nurse needed to
restrain him.
In view of extreme anger & arousal given
IV & IM sedation:
45 mg diazemuls & 20 mg IM haloperidol -
still awake & struggling hard

1.

Notes from my medical records.

Me with Vanessa
Redgrave during
rehearsals for
*Antony and
Cleopatra* in
New York, 1997.

On stage at The Cottesloe
Theatre at the Royal National
Theatre in London, 1997.
I played Othello and Claire
Skinner played Desdemona.

Another scene from
Othello at The
Cottesloe Theatre
with Simon Russell
Beale as Iago.

As Martin Luther King in *The Mountaintop* (2009) at Battersea's Theatre503, with Lorraine Burroughs as Camae.

Still from *Mrs Mandela* (2010) in which I played Nelson Mandela.

Me with Diego Klattenhoff, Morena Baccarin and Mandy Patinkin at the 69th Annual Golden Globe Awards.

Still from *Supergirl* (2015).

Still from *Psychosis and Me* (BBC, 2019).

Chapter Eight

The Collapse of the Young Black Boy

My mind was crumbling and my grip on reality was slipping away. I have absolutely no recollection of actually getting to Camden but at some point, I realised I was standing outside the very shop Martin Luther King had directed me to and unsurprisingly, at three a.m., it was closed. I remember trying to twist the handle to push the doors open. This wasn't supposed to happen. What about all the business of sacrificing myself for the betterment of mankind and closing the gap between good and evil? I was standing outside a clothes shop in north London confused when once again the voice of the great Black icon boomed in my head.

'David. Something's wrong. We need to get you home, I'm sensing danger.'

Fuck.

I remember feeling a little afraid. Suddenly I was cold and tired, I just wanted to get back home, but my feet hurt and I was exhausted. I turned and saw a black cab slowly driving towards me and for some reason I presumed Martin had sent it for me! I flagged it down and jumped in but when the driver asked me 'Where to?' I couldn't remember where I was going.

The voice of Dr King once again came to my assistance. This time with instructions:

'Hold your hands up and I'll beam a message to this man.'

I began making these strange gestures trying to communicate with the driver telepathically. I remember seeing a look of concern in the driver's eyes. The cab slowed down and pulled to the kerb. I don't remember how but I must have got out of it because I found myself sitting on the side of the road and seeing flashing blue police lights reflecting in the windows of the buildings around me and being led to the back of a police van.

This was a wild night, probably the wildest of my entire breakdown. Once in the cell, I was having frightening delusions that every breath I took actually robbed breath from the people I loved. It was really disturbing. Their faces kept appearing in the patterns on the floor, screaming, imploring me not to breathe too deeply as I was taking too much of their air and choking them! An awful night. I think I was screaming a lot and banging on the door. Eventually I blew myself out and slept, but when I woke up in the morning I had absolutely no idea who I was. Martin's voice was gone and in its place was a deafening silence. All of the activity that had kept me awake the night before had vanished. I remember being loaded into the back of another police vehicle and driven to a courthouse, where I was locked up again and after an hour or so put in front of a duty solicitor. The guy was asking me questions about what had happened the night before, but I couldn't remember anything. In fact, I couldn't even tell him my name.

'Where are you from?' he asked.

'I'm from Birmingham.'

'And do you have family?'

'Erm, yes, I have brothers and a sister.'

'And what about your parents?'

'Yes, my mum is there and my dad.'

'What are their names?'

'My mum's name is . . . Mayleen and my dad is called Romeo.'

'Romeo? As in the play?'

'Yes! Wait a minute, I've played Romeo!'

'Played Romeo? Are you an actor?'

'Yes! Yes, I'm an actor! I'm an actor, I trained at RADA . . . what's my name? I had friends, Danny, Jez and Nick. I lived with them . . . David! My name's David!'

What a fucking relief! I felt a bit better now that I had a grasp of who I was. He ran through the charges against me, but I couldn't recall any of it so I just agreed to everything. Shortly after talking with this lawyer I was again handcuffed and taken up some stairs where I found myself in the dock of a magistrate's court. The judge was asking me questions, but I couldn't focus my mind on what he was saying. All I remember seeing was a sea of faces looking at me with this puzzled look. I'm not sure how long I was there but I was soon released from the dock and found myself standing outside the front of the courthouse. It was a bright sunny morning, really beautiful, and the heat was warm on my face. I stood there for a second trying to get my bearings when a lady approached me and asked me if I was okay. I think she must have been in the courtroom because she told me that I'd looked very confused earlier.

'I don't think I'm doing very well,' I said.

She asked me where I lived and again, I couldn't remember but she asked me what Tube station I used and I told her Highbury and Islington. She then flagged down a cab, gave the driver ten pounds and told him to take me there. Amazing that a stranger would take care of me at that moment. If she hadn't appeared, I don't know what would have become of me. I was truly out of my mind at this point: no memory, no delusions, no hallucinations. There was an open chasm where my brain used to be.

After that trip to the clothes shop and brush with the law, the most bizarre night of my life, I got home and crashed out, falling into a deep sleep. Finally, I was woken from a near comatose sleep by the sound of stones hitting my window and voices calling my name. For a moment I thought 'the voices' were back, but it didn't take long to work out where the sound was coming from. I don't know what time it was, although it was bright outside and my curtains were still closed. I slowly walked towards the window, carefully peered out and saw Nick, Jez and Danny standing on the street below. It took me a moment to register them. My mind was blown out, an utter wreck, but I eventually walked to the front door and buzzed them in. They'd been looking for me all night. I really don't remember much about our conversation, I was gone.

After a brief discussion it was decided that Nick and Jeremy would drive me to my mother's place in Birmingham. It was clear I was now very ill and their only option was to get me to a safe environment. Mum's place seemed like the safest bet; however, on the way I began to lose consciousness. Nick jumped into the back of the car and continued to slap me across the face, trying to bring me back to consciousness. In a panic they decided to take me to the closest hospital, which just happened to be Whittington Hospital, where I would spend the next five days lost in some kind of mental maze, from which nobody knew if I would ever recover. Sifting through my medical records, it appears that on certain days I refused to acknowledge who I was and even seemed convinced I was somebody else. Some days I would even give my name as 'Colin' and appear be impersonating my old friend from Birmingham.

Most of those five days are lost to me, just brief flashes remembered. It's clear to me that the young Black boy that I was had simply collapsed. I remember Nick and Jez and Danny and maybe even Jane coming to visit me a couple of times. I recall trying to secretly tell Jez to get me out! I so wanted to get out. I hated where I was. Seeing them on the ward was really odd because I recognised them, but I couldn't make the connection as to why they were there. It was like seeing something familiar but forgetting where you knew it from.

At the time of all this happening to me, I'd never heard of psychosis. It's shocking but the condition had never been explained to me. I was totally confused as to what the hell was happening. Although it would appear from some of my records that the doctors were equally unsure. At one point I was looked at by a neurosurgeon and at another point they considered me to have schizophrenia. The jury was out for quite some time as they worked out how best to deal with me.

Looking back, my actual breakdown probably didn't last very long, but I think I was suffering from the effects of psychosis for months. I'd been isolated since leaving drama school. I had consumed a fair amount of marijuana and I was under a lot of stress and over the course of those first two years, I'd slowly come undone.

Now I was at rock bottom, totally detached from reality and kept in a psychiatric unit on a locked ward. I was considered a danger to myself and possibly others. Short of being arrested by the police, I can't think of many other instances where a person's liberty is taken from them like this. I think this is probably one of the reasons my father was so angry about being sectioned. As far as he was concerned, he was absolutely fine and they'd stolen his freedom and kept him locked up against his will. I was in no such state to debate my liberty. I was lost and acutely unwell. In many ways I'm just lucky that I finally received some treatment. I had no access to my memory when I was sectioned, there was just layer upon layer of confusion. *Is that my hand? Who are all these people? Where am I?* It was a truly disorientating experience that I wouldn't wish on anybody.

Dr Erin Turner, the lead psychiatrist on *Psychosis and Me*, described recovering from my psychotic break as something akin to doing ten years of psychoanalysis in those five days, as I somehow tried to make the right connections in my brain and get back to myself. All I have are the notes. Some days I wouldn't eat or drink. Some days I appeared listless and quiet, other days more energetic and combative. It all remains something of a blur to me but somehow, I got myself through it, found a way back.

My family had travelled down to visit me. They must have been extremely worried seeing me like that but Mum was strong. It was really lovely to spend time with them all. In fact, I got quite upset when they left, and I cried hard.

I felt very broken, like I'd been dissected and taken apart. I couldn't get a grip on exactly what was going on. I was in hospital, but what had happened to me? I now know that the staff had spoken at length to my mother. She had been asked about the family history and had told them of my father's experience, and the stresses of acting and drama school. They pretty much got the whole story.

The records document my mental 'ground zero', the moment everything had come crashing down, and it's no wonder it took me a long to time to actually look at them. It's hard to imagine myself in that broken condition, not making any sense and behaving completely irrationally. That's how powerfully psychosis can rob someone of their faculties. Psychosis left me a shell, unable to comprehend the world around me, with no ability to focus or remember anything. Being given no definition or diagnosis of what was happening to me was also extremely confusing. Had I broken a limb or had a leg amputated, I would have been able to see the problem. I'm sure the doctors would have talked to me about the prognosis, but nobody tried to help me understand what was happening. I was struggling to make sense of everything on my own.

I couldn't work out how best to get myself out of my predicament. One minute my family was there and I recognised some faces, and the next I was alone again in a strange environment, unable to process what was going on. This went on until slowly, over the course of the five days, my condition improved and it was decided that I'd made enough progress to be released into the care of my family. I returned to Birmingham to stay with my mother. I don't really remember very much about this period. I was so keen to get myself back to normal but in reality, I was still very ill, I think. But I was on auto-pilot, being conversant and seemingly normal whilst internally I'd be slipping in and out of focus. But I held it down, kept taking the pills and managed to convince my mum that I was well enough to visit friends. I travelled to the wine bar to see all my old friends. But, though I remember being there, I don't recall what I said to everyone. I think I said some pretty uncomfortable things. I was very uninhibited at this time and had something of a loose tongue. It must have been odd for them to have seen me like that.

During one of these visits to the outside world, I made the fatal mistake of smoking a joint. I don't remember where but as soon as I did, I felt something very strange happening. I went back to my mother's place but this time I couldn't fake my way out of it. I was up in the night, asking Mum odd questions and acting strange. She was getting used to the signs and it wasn't long before she called our family doctor, Dr Coles. He'd been our family doctor my whole life, but seeing him turn up at my mum's flat was weird. Why was he there, at such an odd time? The hallucinations and delusions were not fully back, but I was beginning to get some strange thoughts. After I spoke with him, Dr Coles took my mum to one side and described my mind as being like a spinning clock where the hands on the clock were moving double speed. What was needed was to slow the clock down. He arranged for another short hospital stay.

A couple of days later I remember Mum getting me ready and us both leaving the house to catch a bus. It was a lovely sunny day and I was absolutely convinced that Mum was taking me to be interviewed live on television because I'd managed to make contact with life on another planet and a hastily arranged press conference in front of the world's press was awaiting me. Totally convinced. Me and Mum got off the bus and she walked me down to this building which was actually the Hollymoor Psychiatric Unit in Birmingham but I thought it was a television studio! My mother checked me in, and all the while I was just waiting to be led into a room full of cameras and microphones, the kind that confront movie stars and sportsmen at press junkets. Then I could see Mum collecting her things and saying goodbye to me. I thought she might be going to take her seat in the audience so I didn't think it was unusual, but after an hour or so I thought:

Where's all the international press? There's not much going on in here?

There were no cameras, no interviewers and the place wasn't a television studio. I began to worry.

'Where's my mum?' I asked.

'She'll be along to visit you in a couple of days, David. Why don't you sit yourself down and get comfortable?'

It slowly dawned on me that I was in trouble again, and I automatically went straight to the doors of the ward to try to get out, but I was locked in. That's the moment I realised I'd been sectioned again. How the fuck did that happen? I thought I was doing okay? I sat down and looked around the room. I was the only Black person around, no Black staff or patients. I was alone again in the system. My heart sank around then, and when the nurse came round with her pill trolley I refused to take my medication. After a combative conversation with the duty nurse, a couple of male nurses showed up at the door and I concluded it best to just take the bloody tablets. I knew the presence of these two guys wasn't a good sign. I took two tablets and went to lie down and the next thing I knew I was fast asleep.

Chapter Nine

The Ward

Waking up in a mental institution is a strange and bizarre experience made only slightly more bearable by the drugs administered the night before arrival. It's an odd sensation to come round on a mental ward – in this case the Hollymoor Psychiatric Hospital in Birmingham – and not recognise your own body. It took a while for my hands, feet and legs to understand that they were attached to my body. I just lay there for an hour trying to make sense of what was going on. I knew I was awake and alive, but that was as far as I could make out. I repeatedly wriggled my fingers and toes to be sure they hadn't been removed. Once I was 100 per cent certain that all of me seemed present and correct, I turned my attention to opening my eyes. My eyelids felt like forty-pound kettle bells and they absolutely refused to stay open. After a minute or two, they settled into a thousand-yard stare as my brain tried its best to focus and understand what all these people were doing in my fucking bedroom.

Slowly it started to come together, and I realised I was on the locked ward of a psychiatric hospital. Certainly not the best start to the day for sure and the realisation hit hard. As my eyes began to focus, it was the decor that they settled on first. The crusty walls, the bedding and the parquet flooring came in for particular scrutiny as I cast a disapproving glance at my surroundings.

When did I decide to move in here? Oh, that's right. This was my second trip into a mental institution.

I've been sectioned TWICE!

I must be pretty good at this.

My sense of smell was last to wake up and, eventually, I noticed the distinct smell of piss coming from the bed next to me. I turned my head slowly and caught a glimpse of the mouth-breather in the adjacent bed who hadn't woken up yet. I gazed at him for what seemed like an eternity, trying to figure out how the hell I had ended up in a bed next to this guy.

I was sure I was an actor before this. I was absolutely sure of it!

I studied at a really good drama school, had lots of mates and laughed a lot.

What the fuck had happened?

My disdain for the environment intensified. The dodgy art on the walls, the fixtures and fittings – everything looked grim. I wished to God I was still asleep and, indeed, soon enough I was.

I was awake again. Sunlight creeping through the drab curtains and more noise and movement now. Patients were starting to wander about murmuring, and I could see breezy nurses prepping trolleys full of bottles and pills in the corner of the room. *No, this is no time for sleep. I need to get my arse out of bed.* I noticed the mouth-breather in the bed next to me had gone, he was already up and about, and I was momentarily filled with shame as I realised he'd probably woken up and looked at me in the same way I'd looked at him, thinking:

What the hell am I doing in the bed next to this *guy?*

As I tried to gather my thoughts, the inner dialogue started to activate and then the usual chatter began, performing its confusing daily pantomime. But something was different today, there was something I needed to remember.

What was it?

My brother had visited the day before. I remembered because he had become quite upset with me when I tried communicating with him by singing the 'Welcome' tune the scientists in the movie *Close Encounters of the Third Kind* had played to the alien spaceships when they landed at the end of the movie. My brother was not impressed. He'd said something to me that was really important, though. What was it?

'David, if you want to get out of here, you've got to start acting normal.'

Acting normal? Well, I'm an actor. I know I can act! I've got to start acting like a normal person, not a mental patient. That's how I'm going to get out. So, I'm going to get up right now and brush my teeth because that's normal behaviour. Get the fuck up and start behaving like a person who doesn't belong in a mental institution.

I sat up in bed and took a moment. I needed to plan what I was about to do because my head felt like it was swimming in jelly and I wasn't sure where my toothbrush was exactly. Mum came yesterday and she brought me some new kit. Maybe it was in the cabinet next to my bed? I swung my legs out of the bed and glanced down at the cabinet. Again, for some reason, there was an elaborate conversation in my head about the decor and how there wasn't enough space on the cabinet shelf and how the handle on the door was broken.

There was a comb and a half-full cup of water, a magazine and a white plastic bag that presumably held my toiletries, but it all looked a mess. There were too many things on that shelf. I reached slowly down to grab the white plastic bag and look inside, and there was indeed a toothbrush and some toothpaste, along with some moisturiser and tissues, all the stuff mums pack for their boys when they're spending the night away. It was all there. Normally brushing your teeth would take around two to three minutes. Under the influence of Chlorpromazine (the antipsychotic drug), however, I discovered that brushing my teeth would now take me forty minutes to an hour. Even taking a single step was difficult, walking in a straight line even more so. Navigating my way to the bathroom wasn't easy and, once there, catching a glimpse of my rather puffy face and unkempt appearance did little to spur my soul. I looked fucking dreadful. It took a while to figure out that the person looking at me in the mirror was, in fact, me.

After a moment or two that perhaps lasted twenty minutes, I took the toothbrush out of the bag and got to work. Getting the toothpaste onto the brush was the next hurdle. My hands couldn't grip the brush. I couldn't get the paste out of the tube and when it did finally come out, it went everywhere. Another few minutes were spent trying to wipe up the mess before I finally settled on the idea of just dipping the brush into the paste that was already in the sink and trying to make my way from there. This worked well and I was finally ready to brush my teeth. Then came the second hurdle – I couldn't find my mouth with the toothbrush. I think I must have brushed both my nostrils and my left ear before I finally got the damn brush into my mouth and started to vigorously wiggle it about in my gob. I did this for about ten minutes, not sure why, but I wanted everyone to see me doing it, the nurses in particular. If I could prove I was normal, I would get out of there faster. This was my mission – act normal, get out. When I was convinced that everyone on the ward had seen me brushing my face, I decided to head back to my bed to tidy up my space. I moved a few things around on the cabinet, straightened my slippers and smiled at everybody that happened to look in my direction.

I glanced around the room. Mouth-breather was now dressed and randomly measuring distances on the floor. The distance between a stain on the floor and his bed, the distance from his bed to his shoes. He'd measure all sorts of spaces and make a mental note to himself once he'd completed each task. I watched him for quite some time, completely enthralled. People-watching is a particular joy of the acting process and even in there, on this ward and in my confused and sedated state, I found it fascinating. I was the only Black patient on the ward; most of the other patients were white and of a range of ages. There was a beautiful Indian girl who was frail and fairylike who always stood facing the wall. She only moved when someone got too close to her. There was also a creepy guy I ended up naming 'Iago' because he wouldn't leave me alone. One day I happened to fall asleep in a chair, as I often did, and I woke up to find him licking my ear! Well, that gave me a hell of a shock. I couldn't gather my thoughts enough to tell him to fuck off at the time, so I instead gave him serious vibes for the following couple of days. He ended up leaving me alone.

My toothbrushing routine became my secret escape plan and it started each day on a positive note and demonstrated that I was cognisant of personal hygiene and aware enough of my surroundings to make my way around the ward and back to bed. It became a daily performance and, even under the influence of the anti-psychotic drugs, I did my absolute best to catch the eye of everyone I saw. Wake up, brush my teeth, say good morning to all the nurses and pretend to read the magazine my mother had brought in. All totally normal behaviour.

But then came the wall calendar incident. If anyone were to make a movie of my life, this moment would go down as the greatest in escape planning since Sylvester Stallone took one for the team and broke his arm in the movie *Escape to Victory*!

It was around day five of my Shawshank plan to get off the mental ward, five straight days of slow-motion, normal behaviour. After returning from brushing my teeth I slumped down on my bed ready to do the usual tidying up act when something caught my eye. Across the room, on a wall next to a noticeboard, was a wall calendar, garishly painted and seemingly designed by a two-year-old. It was rather large and something about it bothered me. I stared at it for about ten minutes trying to figure out what it was until finally it hit me.

It says Wednesday?

The wall calendar . . . it says it's Wednesday.

Now, drugs or no drugs, I knew full well that the evening before the rather lovely nurse that came around at 'pill time' said something to me about it being Wednesday. What was it she said?

'Thursday tomorrow, one day closer to the weekend and I can have a couple of days off. Do us a favour and take your medicine for me, there's a love.'

The wheels in my head began to turn (very slowly). If I went to sleep after taking my tablets . . . and I've just brushed my teeth . . . today must be Thursday?

I looked again at the wall calendar. It had the wrong date!

By now some of the nurses had gathered at their stations after their morning rounds, chatting and casting an eye over the patients. Nearly everybody was awake now, either wandering around or sitting on their beds, but *nobody* had spotted the date on the wall calendar. A voice in my head said:

'Go and change the fucking day now before someone else does!'

Now, you have to imagine this in slow motion because nothing is easy under the influence of antipsychotics, but I stood up, stretched and yawned all casual like, doing my best to attract the attention of all the staff. I walked over to the wall calendar, slotted out the WEDNESDAY card and then replaced it with THURSDAY.

It was all very casually done but I tell you, I felt like I'd just completed a Rubik's Cube with my arsehole. I stood there feeling like a genius. I was absolutely chuffed and one or two of the nurses actually nodded in approval. Fuckin' get in! It was like scoring the winning goal in a World Cup final. That was the morning I added 'Calendar Monitor' to my escape plan. Get up, brush teeth, tidy space, CHANGE WALL CALENDAR. My plan was really taking shape now and to make sure I didn't ruin it, for the rest of the day I worked really hard to behave myself and not annoy or get up in anyone's face:

'What's in these tablets you're giving me?'

'Why do I have to take them?'

'Are you drugging me?'

I kept a lid on all of it.

Just take what you're given and shut the fuck up. Don't challenge anybody or question anything.

Looking back to my first hospitalisation, I recognise that I was probably quite a handful. I was distressed and frightened and, had it not been for my drama school friends Nick and Jez, God knows what would have become of me. This time, here I was again, a large Black man, with a big voice always asking twenty questions about the medicine I was taking. Once or twice I'd notice a male nurse or two lurking by the door, presumably ready to step in should things get out of hand. But I just wanted to know what was going on. When I was eventually released, Mum remarked that our family doctor, Dr Coles, had commented:

'We're lucky that David isn't a violent boy. He's acting out a lot but it's all harmless and that's a very good thing.'

Lucky me. Many people, particularly men of colour, have lost their lives being restrained in mental institutions. After my documentary aired I twice met people in the street, both complete strangers, who had approached to tell me of their personal experiences of family members who had lost their lives that way. An Indian man described how his brother who had had several psychotic episodes lost his life whilst being restrained and a Black woman told me of her uncle who died in the same manner. Both times I cried. It was so odd, strangers telling you their most intimate stories in the street, in broad daylight, and each time the pair of us sobbing about it. Deep down I was also thinking how easily that could have been me. So yes, I guess I was a very lucky boy.

Now, two weeks into my stay, my mother, who visited me at the hospital most days, arrived with a particularly big smile on her face.

'We're going home!' she said. 'You've been doing really well, they tell me, and you can leave here and carry on your treatment with me back at the flat.'

'Okay, Mum,' I said. 'That'll be better, I think.'

So Mum packed up all my things, put the stuff I had in my cabinet and took some clothes out of a bag she'd brought with her. I recognised the clothes: they were mine all right, but they still felt strange. I hadn't seen my own clothes for ages, and I'd been spending most days in pyjamas. It actually took a while for me to get dressed. Mum helped me get ready. It felt weird, and I couldn't really understand why she was helping me put my clothes on and why I couldn't get my arms into the sleeves or do the zip up on my trousers, much less tie my shoelaces. But I was going home, and I had to get ready. That was all I understood.

It's important to know that at this point, a few weeks into my stay at Hollymoor Hospital, nobody had actually told me what was wrong with me or what had happened in my breakdown or what the prognosis was. I genuinely had no idea what was going on. Because of all the drugs I'd been given, my brain felt like it had been pulled out through my eyeballs, put in a blender and fed back to me in a smoothie. Prior to my hospitalisation, my thoughts were vivid and strange, and there was a kind of electricity flowing through me that was actually rather exciting. Now there was a dull silence and I could hardly string two words together. It felt like someone had switched off the power. But I was going home, finally, and that was all that mattered.

I hadn't once left the hospital grounds since I'd arrived, so walking through the gates and onto the public streets for the first time felt extremely odd. I was heavily sedated and still felt like my brain was swilling about in a bag of oil, but now I was walking down the street with my mother. She was overjoyed to have me coming home and, even though I wasn't really at the races, it felt good to be out and in her company. I remember getting on the bus with her and taking my seat towards the back downstairs, sort of oblivious to all the passengers around me. Nobody was staring at me. It wasn't as if I had a sign over my head that said:

I've just come out of a mental institution.

I was just another passenger on the bus and it was a relief. In truth, I think I've taken much of the feeling that day into my professional life. I'm just happy to be working, earning a living from acting. I sometimes forget about the aspects of fame that come with the job so that it can be a jolt when someone in Tesco knows my name and seems genuinely chuffed to meet me. I'm often momentarily thrown by it.

Mum chatted the whole way back to the flat. She asked me how I was and I did my best to answer, but I wasn't very talkative. I just stared out through the glass on my side of the bus, watching all the people we were passing. Watching strangers doing their shopping, minding their own business, people who hadn't been on a locked ward or antipsychotic drugs. They were just normal, everyday people milling about. I felt envious of them. I yearned to have my senses back so I could wander around not feeling lost and confused. I just wanted to be like them.

Even though people think my profession is about standing out and getting noticed, I often find it deeply uncomfortable to put myself in the 'tits and teeth' frame of mind. There's a part of me that sees right through it and on the odd occasion I'm on a red carpet I have to work very hard not to skip the flashing bulbs altogether. I can remember doing red carpets when *Homeland* hit big, watching Claire Danes and Damian Lewis look so comfortable as the photographers called out their names and the cameras flashed in a sea of light. I'd never seen anything like it. Once or twice I'd make my way through the kitchens to avoid the experience, anything to swerve that bit of show pony 'me time'. I've got better at it over the years but it took some getting used to. I guess once you've pissed yourself in a mental institution, it's a little difficult to ever believe you're the dog's bollocks!

I stayed with Mum for about three or four weeks after being released, continuing to take my meds and sleeping lots throughout the day and night. I knew I hadn't yet completely recovered from whatever had happened, but I was doing my best to get myself back to normal, back to some semblance of the old David and possibly return to London to continue my acting career. One time I recall being woken by my mother because someone had called to see how I was doing. It was a director that I'd worked with at RADA, Norman Jones, who'd heard about my breakdown and just wanted to say hi and offer a friendly voice of support. I was still so out of it, though, that I couldn't work out who he was. I listened as he introduced himself on the phone and tried to jog my memory of the play we had done together, but I couldn't get my mind to work. I shook my head and handed the phone back to my mother before going back to sleep. Mum apologised for me, but it just illustrated how far from normal I still was. Years later, I was sitting at home when Norman's name and photo appeared on the TV. He'd passed away. A sense of sadness came over me in that moment as I realised I never did get chance to thank him for calling me that day. The memory had become lost in the fog of my brain only to be brought back when I'd heard his name said again.

As the days and weeks passed my daytime routine fell into a familiar pattern, starting with a bit of *Richard and Judy* and progressing on through the daytime telly shows till the afternoon when my mother allowed me to take a stroll up to the corner shop to hire a video from the Indian newsagent's. I began binge-watching '80s action movies like *Terminator* and *Beverly Hills Cop*, movies where the actor's name was often above the title. Stallone, Tom Cruise, Arnie! The afternoons became blockbuster time and I allowed myself to once again dream about resuming my career as an actor.

Lui came to take me out one afternoon. We played pitch and putt at some local place Lui knew. I remember it was a beautiful, sunny day that day, and though I tried my best to be funny, I couldn't quite manage it. My brain just couldn't click into gear. Lui was great, he just talked away all day and drove me round before taking me home in the evening. It was so nice being out. The contrast with being indoors all day taking these drugs couldn't have been more drastic. I wanted to be normal again, to get going, get my mind sharp and return to acting. I was very down, frustrated by the lethargy in my thinking and movement. I'd sit indoors all day. There wasn't much follow-up from the doctors and I was just stuck in this endless cycle of pills, sleep and fogginess.

Mum watched me like a hawk throughout this whole period, keeping a close eye to see if I was keeping it together or spinning out of control. I was well aware of what she was doing. Again, the line between my personal behaviour and performance blurred as I knew if I was ever going to get back to my career in London, I'd have to convince Mum that all was well. I tried hard to appear sane and in control but I began to struggle with the antipsychotic drugs I was taking. They were starting to have a very negative effect on my state of my mind. I was hugely overweight and my general movement slow and laboured. Concerned by this, Mum called the hospital and spoke to somebody on the psychiatric ward and explained that my medication was making me depressed. She was told I could stop taking it, just like that, and one of their specialists would be in touch for a follow-up or some such vague pronouncement.

I had taken the medication diligently every day and imagined that only my recovery lay ahead. Surely not taking these tablets would bring back my zest and sharpness? So the next day, with Mum's consent, I stopped taking the antipsychotics. I was fine for a couple of days. There didn't seem to be any major changes in my behaviour, but four or five days later I was beginning to feel a familiar rush of energy, a euphoria that I'd experienced before. I so desperately wanted to get my life back to normal and continue with my career that instead of coming clean to Mum, I hid this sudden surge and pretended as though all was well. Knowing that I was being watched so closely only added to the drama as I did my best to act normal. But deep down inside, as the days passed,

I could feel my mind spinning faster and faster. Those drugs had been a hand brake on my racing thoughts and without them I was once again beginning to lose control. I did a great job of hiding all this from my mum because I thought if I told her the truth, she'd never let me get back to London.

Finally, I convinced my mother to let me travel to London for the day, just to catch up with some friends, and was surprised when she said that she thought it was a good idea. The following week I set off but I don't remember anything about the journey. Once out of my mum's reach I must have stopped trying to hide all the changes I was experiencing and as soon as I got to London, I once again became disorientated. Somehow, I found my way to an ex-girlfriend's place and I stayed there for a couple of days until one morning my mum walked into her house. I knew I'd fucked up. The chemicals in my brain had once again got the better of me, but this time, having witnessed what had happened, my mother was more prepared. She gave me half a tablet as soon as I got home, another half a couple of days later and she slowly reduced the size of the pill she was giving me until finally she wasn't giving me any pills at all. Mum knew best. It had taken some time but at last I felt I had balanced out. Nobody from the hospital ever checked in to see how I was doing, there were no calls, I didn't have a follow-up meeting with anybody. Mum just weaned me off the tablets and I have never needed a single tablet since. The madness was gone.

I remained in Birmingham, at my mum's place, for another couple of weeks before I again got that old familiar feeling . . .

Maybe I don't belong here?

Mum was obviously reluctant to see me leave and get back to my life in London. She'd almost become convinced that it was 'acting', and in particular Shakespeare, that had sent me crazy in the first place! At one point I thought she'd never let me out of her sight again. But with a little convincing, she relented and after I'd had several successful visits to friends and re-engaged with my agent, her fears began to subside. I really wanted to get back to my life. I'd had a hell of an experience, but through it all I had maintained the outlook that all this would prove beneficial at some point. I don't know how but I felt that such an extreme event had to hold within it something of value for me.

The Chinese symbol for 'crisis' is actually composed of two characters, one signifying 'danger' and the other 'opportunity'. I believed that buried in my experience was an opportunity for renewal, a chance to reset and build from a different perspective. I'd had a wild summer, but under my mother's care back in Birmingham I'd recovered. Now it was time to fly the nest once more. I was together. I felt it. I returned to London, moving into a gorgeous little three-bed house in West Hampstead with my old friend Danny and Paudge, another former RADA student, who had just left college and was now looking for a place to live and launch his career in the business. We lived not far from the Heath and all got on like a house on fire. The place was a riot, again lots of laughter and fun times. It felt great to be back in London, living life on my own terms.

Although I'd been through a traumatic experience, rather than dwell on what I had gone through I simply revelled in the life that I had. I was enjoying being back in London, and it didn't take long for me to get my first acting gig at the Theatre Royal Stratford East, one of the most vibrant and entertaining venues in town, then under the leadership of artistic director Philip Hedley. This would become the place where I would finally experience joy on stage, something I'd been searching for since I'd left drama school. I was cast as the Prince's confidant in a production of *Cinderella* in one of the theatre's famous Christmas pantomimes. I'd never had so much fun on a professional stage!

One of the things that makes a venue so special is the audience. Whilst the house was packed with kids in the daytime, in the evening there was plenty for the adults to enjoy. On some nights after Christmas, when there wasn't a kid in the house, we had some of the best shows and the biggest laughs of the entire run. It felt great to be enjoying acting again. I was also less aware of the white gaze, and I felt free, easing myself slowly back into my career in a way that suited me. I no longer felt like a green young thing and, strangely enough, my experience of being so unwell had almost grounded me. Still, I was aware that I wasn't fully back to my confident self just yet. I had no idea if the actors I was working with knew that I was recovering from a breakdown. I presumed rumours were circulating but there were no overt signs from anybody.

Not long afterwards I got a gig at the National Theatre Studio working on a piece called *Black Poppies*, a collection of real-life stories from Black British soldiers who recounted their experiences of racism and discrimination after putting their lives on the line fighting for England. It was a powerful piece. Once again, I had chosen to do a play primarily about the Black experience, but there was no fear of exposing myself to old insecurities because they'd all been smashed. I was building a whole new personality, slowly putting new pieces of myself together whilst I moved further and further away from the deluded car crash I had been the year before. It's only looking back on it now that I realise I simply put the whole thing behind me and got on with my life and career. I hardly even gave my breakdown a thought. It just became a tale I'd tell from time to time. I didn't dwell on its significance. In truth, I didn't have time.

I was back in the groove in London, criss-crossing the town like back in the old days, but there was a new awareness about me. It hadn't been a year since I'd been on the ward, walking barefoot across the parquet floor, and now I was working with a group of fantastic Black actors at the National Theatre Studio and having the time of my life. I was thriving amongst these young, talented Black men. Every day the humour and rapport of the group was a joy to be around. The actors were all very different in their own ways but their confidence and sense of identity made a huge impression on me. Black and British like me, they lacked the insecurities that I'd suffered, and they had an ease about them that was striking. The more time I spent in their company, the better I began to feel about myself.

Several of the cast – Gary MacDonald, Robbie Gee, Michael Buffong, Roger Griffiths and Sylvester Williams – all belonged to a very talented and funny comedy group called The Posse, writing and directing their own work and putting on raucous shows at the Theatre Royal Stratford East. I remember going over to the theatre one night to see them perform and I'd never seen an audience like it: young, predominately Black and extremely vocal. I had as much fun as the audience. The performance captured the essence of Black British humour, a combination of clever writing built around the cultural themes of the day. The resulting laughter had the place rocking. The jokes came thick and fast and the whole evening seemed to bless me with a sense of community and belonging I hadn't experienced before.

I became particularly close with the actor Gary MacDonald, the most extraordinarily confident and uniquely funny Black man I'd ever met. We had so much fun together exploring London's vibrant club scene each weekend, buzzing through the night as the music played and all the beautiful people moved and swayed around us. One day Gary told me 'The Posse' were about to do another gig back at the Theatre Royal, a very funny Black take on Charles Dickens' novella *A Christmas Carol* called *Pinchy Cobie and the Seven Duppies*. They'd be performing in London before taking the show on a national tour. Playing Scrooge, or 'Pinchy', was the brilliant Eddie Nestor (now a BBC London radio presenter) and rounding out the group was singer/songwriter and actor Victor Romero Evans, a gorgeous man, super talented and as authentic as they come – rooted in his Blackness and unapologetically fabulous. The actor Brian Bovell, an original member of The Posse, was engaged on another project and Gary asked me if I would step in for him and do the show. I leaped at the opportunity. My agent was a little perplexed when I told her, but it was important for me. This wasn't just another gig; these guys were helping me reconstruct my identity and being around them was a great help in me putting myself back together.

Rehearsals went well. There was a bit of ribbing from the other guys, that I was 'classically trained' and from RADA, but it was all very light-hearted. Most of these guys had come up through youth groups and had found their own way into acting one way or another and one or two of them appeared in popular television shows of the day. Robbie Gee was appearing in the Channel Four show *Desmond's* starring the wonderful Norman Beaton, the Guyanese actor who was one of the only Black actors of the day to have his own show. For the first time in my career I had cool, confident people to look up to and I was no longer the only Black guy in the room. It's impossible to overestimate how much this helped me as I sought to piece together my fragmented psyche.

Chapter Ten

The Dreams of the Young Black Boy

The five stages in the life of an actor, according to American actress Mary Astor:

1. Who's David Harewood?
2. Get me David Harewood.
3. Get me a David Harewood type.
4. Get me a young David Harewood.
5. Who's David Harewood?

If there was one person who always had the ability to pick me up when I was feeling low and give me confidence when I was down, it was my best friend Lui. From the moment I told him I was going to be an actor at seventeen years old he was always totally convinced that I was going to be successful. He never, ever doubted it and was a constant source of encouragement. I would often call him back in those early days whenever I was feeling a little frustrated and after a good chat on the phone, I'd always see things from a different perspective.

'Dave, trust me. Might take you a while, but you're gonna make it. No doubt in my mind, son. Absolutely none.'

Whatever role I had, he'd say it was just a stepping stone to something greater and that I just had to hang in there because it was definitely going to happen for me. By the time I'd put the phone down, I felt like a million dollars. Lui's belief in me lifted me up, giving me the sense of value I so often lacked.

Once I'd fully re-established myself in the business, I had a far deeper understanding of how difficult it was going to be for me to be successful in the UK. For years there had been a steady stream of American shows depicting Black life with rounded characters that not only challenged stereotypes and entertained but also shed light on the issues of the day. But there was no equivalent on the English side of the pond. I grew frustrated with the narrow range of characters I was offered.

Don't get me wrong, I was pretty busy, always popping up on the telly playing a lawyer or a policeman or a soldier or a boxer – the standard fare. I always did my best with whatever I had. But I had the sense that I was treading water and not progressing on to more complex and expressive characters, particularly on screen. I wanted to get my teeth into something more substantive, but those opportunities simply weren't open to me.

Luckily for me, my first agent, Pat Marmont, was a firm believer that a fully rounded actor's career should be built from the stage, so I peppered my one-dimensional television work with some meaty roles in the theatre. I was always able to flex my acting muscles on stage and so it was never too long before I was back treading the boards. I loved the whole ritual of doing a play: rehearsals, getting familiar with the cast, diving into the text, learning all the moves with props and tape on the floor marking out the parameters of the set, and finally edging towards the dress rehearsal and the first performance. Before you know it, you're sitting in your dressing room listening to the audience slowly filling up the auditorium and it's showtime! I found the process magical and always took the opportunity be a part of it whenever I could.

I tried my best to keep showing my range and stepping into TV sitcoms as well, giggling my way through the day working with Dawn French, Kathy Burke and Harry Enfield. One of my personal favourites was *Game On* with Samantha Janus, Ben Chaplin and Matthew Cottle. *Game On* was filmed in front of a live audience, so my theatre training came in handy when it came to my live segment. I had so much fun surfing the laughter from the audience just as I'd watched my heroes do as a child. But as always, after the gig was done nothing particularly exciting happened. I was still in the same place and moving on to the next encounter. Around me some of my drama school friends, who happened to be white, were getting great roles: juicy leads or edgy villains. The 'green-eyed monster' got me once or twice. I'd hate myself for it afterwards, but I knew it wasn't my friends that I was jealous of, it was just their opportunities.

Around this time, I was invited by my agent to take part in a workshop in which a group of eight up-and-coming young script writers would get together with an established director and, over the course of a week, each would write a scene to be performed and directed on the Friday evening. It was a five-day job, the thinking being that actors were around good new writers and a talented young director. I thought:

Yeah, sure, I'll have some of that. It's something different and might keep things interesting.

I received the instructions a few days later and jumped on the train, heading out into the plush green wilds of Kent. It was a beautiful ride on a bright sunny day and I had tunes playing on my Walkman. Soon I disembarked at a little tin-pot train station and made my way outside to get a cab. Naturally, I'm a city person and at home in the busy streets, but once in the countryside my Spidey-senses were tingling. I eventually made my way to the location after a long drive through some proper smart neighbourhoods, which ended when we turned down a side road opening up into a beautiful courtyard with a converted barn on one side that had a huge glass extension built onto it and a row of guest cottages.

It was a really nice group of people, we had a lively welcome dinner where wine flowed and the next day we got to work. By midday, scripts were arriving, pages of dialogue that the actors would be asked to read and work on. There were five actors: three men and two women, so most of the writers created scenes either between a man and a woman or two men. We were all pretty busy reading and working on scripts and every evening we'd eat together and talk things through with the writers. The director would drop pearls of wisdom from the end of the table. It was all very civilised.

I was the only Black person there that week. In fact, I'd put a bet on it that I was the only Black person within a country mile of the place. In the confines of the rehearsal space, I felt okay but most lunchtimes, rather than head into town with the others, I'd stay and snack from the on-site cafe. I preferred to just munch down a sandwich and wait for the free dinner. I'm not sure why I didn't go with the others but my Spidey-senses had a tickle that something might be amiss, so I stayed put in the main house. On the Thursday evening, after dinner was served, the director was holding court and explaining to the writers that the next day they would be seeing their work performed and I remember he said:

'So, when you eventually write your film, you must always remember that you may write your main character as tall and blonde and the most striking person ever seen, but the actual actor or actress cast in the role may not look exactly as you would have imagined. So you should be prepared for that.'

I thought about what he'd said for a second and I shot back, 'They might be Black!'

There was silence around the table, not an awkward one, but one where I could hear brains turning over.

The director said, 'I'm not sure about that. I think that's adding a whole different issue. I think that's changing the scene completely.'

'I don't follow you,' I said.

'Well, unless you're actually writing a Black character ... I would presume if they were writing the character, they would say he was Black?'

I said, 'Do you not think a Black actor could be cast in a non-specific role?'

'I guess you could, but it would change the whole dynamic of the piece,' he shot back.

The whole thing suddenly got a bit lively. Some of the writers agreed that they should specify that such and such a character is Black whilst others disagreed and stuck to the original point, which was that in the casting process, if the best actor was Black, they wouldn't have a problem. It was a healthy back and forth and being the only Black person in the room, it was interesting to hear the different views.

One writer said, 'I don't actually know many Black people, so I probably wouldn't write any Black characters specifically because I sort of feel I don't know what I'm talking about.'

It was a most revealing evening.

At the end of the night I headed to bed, but I had a sense it had been an uncomfortable evening for some. Maybe as a result of the conversation at least half of the writers asked me to work on their scripts the next day as the lead male, much to the annoyance of the director, who hardly spoke to me. At lunchtime the gang once again headed into town but, as it was the last day, I decided to go with them. We all piled into a taxi and made our way into the town centre. It was a lovely little place, but as I went with the gang into the first couple of shops to look around, I could see the shock of the people inside at the sight of me. One old guy was actually following me and watching me in the most obvious way so, in the end, I just said to the others that I'd wait outside. Nobody had noticed and I didn't want to cause a scene. My Spidey-senses were proper tingling now. When the group came out of the shop, they decided to pop into one more place but again I chose to wait outside as I couldn't be bothered to deal with the hassle. Once when they were inside, I looked up and saw a police car driving by slowly and I thought, *Here we go.* A minute later the car passed me going the opposite way, again driving slowly. I looked in the shop window hoping the other actors would be on their way out, but it was too late. The police car pulled up in front of me and out climbed a rather stout officer.

'Can I help you?' said the copper.

'Not really. No,' I said.

'Can I ask you what you're doing around here? Don't see many of your lot around here.'

'My lot?'

'Look, lad, I'm just asking you some questions. No need for the sarcasm. What are you doing in town?'

'I'm an actor and I'm doing a workshop with a group of other people. Some of them are in that shop and I'm just waiting for them.'

'Oh, you're an actor? Well, you're not acting very normal, are you?'

'Excuse me?'

Just then the others stepped outside and saw me being questioned and they were absolutely furious, and I mean furious. They got 'full posh' on the copper, saying how outrageous it was, that they wanted his number, they were going to make a complaint. In the end I had to tell them to calm down. I'm not sure if any of them had ever been spoken to by police so it was interesting observing them in this situation. It was a very quiet ride back to the house because they'd been going into town the whole week with no issues at all and the minute I went with them they'd encountered trouble. Those actors had probably spent more time thinking about the reality of life as a person of colour in the last twelve hours than they ever had before. They couldn't stop apologising, which I told them was completely unnecessary, and then we returned to the barn to finish off the workshop. I remember leaving thinking that the problem of me getting on in the business was far more complex than I'd imagined. I called up Lui and again he propped me up, telling me that in time things would be different.

'Dave, they can't see it yet, but trust me, in time they will and you'll be laughing,' he said.

Around this time, Lui's sister, Silvana, was getting married in Italy and the pair of us decided that we'd drive through Europe, the Swiss Alps and down into Italy to attend the wedding and then drive home. We had the most fantastic trip. Lui could speak at least three languages, so we were never in any trouble. We enjoyed it so much that from then on we drove over every year and would spend the entire month of August camping out in various sites and driving down the Amalfi Coast. It was so good to be around Lui.

Chapter Eleven

Go West, Young Black Man

Life was good. Another couple of years rolled by, when one afternoon I got a call from my agent to tell me that Corin and Vanessa Redgrave were about to do two new productions, one of *Julius Caesar* and another of *Antony and Cleopatra*, with Vanessa playing Cleopatra and Corin playing Caesar. I'd obviously heard of the two powerhouse actors and I was keen to find out more. *Antony and Cleo* would play in London before a spell in a couple of places in the UK and then a tour to Italy and Brazil. Both productions would then play in rep at a theatre in Houston, Texas. It sounded like a fabulous tour, but when I found out what parts they wanted me to play I was even more keen. Corin wanted me to play Marc Antony and Vanessa wanted me to play Enobarbus. Not only would I be working with legendary actors but the parts I had were brilliant. I signed up!

Antony would be played by a Black American actor with the rest of the cast made up from an international group with a sprinkling of British talent. We began rehearsing and opened the production at the Riverside Studios in Hammersmith. I found the character of Enobarbus wonderful fun and he has a famous speech, referred to as 'The Barge' speech, and it was one of the most beautiful speeches I'd ever had the pleasure of delivering on stage. I also found it fascinating to watch Vanessa at work. She would sometimes come on from different entrances, wearing different costumes from what she'd worn the night before! She was constantly inventing and making her character truly live in the moment. Her performances were stunning. In contrast, though, her Antony seemed to be struggling. He just couldn't remember his lines and found it difficult keeping up with Vanessa's 'inventive' playing. We were all of the opinion that the tour wouldn't be going forward because it didn't appear that the American actor was very settled. At the end of the London run, I was convinced that would be it.

A couple of weeks slipped by with no news and then, one day I'll never forget, I was driving down the Euston Road when my mobile phone rang. I picked it up and it was Vanessa Redgrave. I was very surprised to get her call. There was a bit of small talk before she told me that unfortunately she'd lost her Antony as he'd decided he didn't want to continue, but then she asked me:

'So, I was thinking, David, would *you* play Antony in his place?'

I nearly crashed the car. What? Me play Antony opposite Vanessa Redgrave? I told her I'd discuss it with my agent. To my surprise, my agent didn't think it was a good idea, but I didn't listen. I was all in. I'd been waiting for an opportunity to do something out of the box and having the chance to pair up with one of the most famous actresses on the planet was a chance I couldn't miss.

Vanessa and I had a blast working together. We were able to generate much more energy in the roles. At one point she decided that we should physically fight on stage so the two of us were rolling around on the ground trying to throttle each other. One night

I accidently caught her and we bumped heads. I gave her a bad bruise over her eye and we calmed it down after that. She was incredible to work with, a legend. How could I possibly have turned down a chance like that? For what? Another policeman on the telly? A footballer accused of a violent crime?

We took the play to Verona, a beautiful city, and performed on a stage in the ruins of a Roman theatre. Members of the audience sat on cushions under the stars. It was a magical setting. After the show, Vanessa took us all to a local restaurant where we were plied with *vongole* and wine. The little Italian I knew from Lui seemed to thrill the staff and we were chatting and laughing until late in the evening when the grappa came out, a lethal concoction that got us all totally hammered. The next stop was Brazil, before Vanessa and a few of the others, including myself, joined Corin and his company in Houston, Texas, to run the productions together.

This was the first time I'd ever been to the US. I remember all the formality at the border, handing in my passport and the officer looking at it and saying:

'O-1 Visa?'

I said, 'I'm sorry?'

'You have an O-1 Visa.'

'Is that okay?'

'Yeah, yeah, it's very okay. You're a person with extraordinary abilities. What do you do?'

'I'm an actor.'

'Are you in a TV show?'

'No. I'm doing a play at a theatre here.'

'Well, you must be pretty good. Have a good day, sir.'

And he tossed my passport back through the glass.

I immediately noticed the number of people of colour around in uniform working; they all looked so confident.

We joined up with the new company and set about staging the two shows. In order to get paid I had to go and open a local bank account, so I made my way to a bank near the theatre and told them what I wanted to do. 'Yes, just wait in the room on your right and the manager will be in to see you shortly.'

I waited in the room. After about five minutes this young Black girl walked in, roughly same age as me, and asked me if she could help me. I said:

'I'm just waiting for the manager.'

She said, 'Yes. That's me!'

She could tell by the fact that my eyes nearly popped out of my head that I was surprised and she laughed.

'Haven't you ever seen a Black female bank manager?'

'Erm . . . no,' I said.

We chuckled and talked about life and things. I was telling her about London and she was telling me her story and soon we got the account details up and running and I was a paid man in America. I bought a bike, a big cruiser in a laid-back style with beautiful curves. I sailed down those streets, under that big old sky with the sun setting slowly on the day, listening to 'Cruisin'' by D'Angelo on my Walkman.

What a tune.

I really hit it off with the actor who was now playing Enobarbus: Alex Morris, a wonderful Black actor. He would often invite me over to his family cookouts, where neighbours and friends would swing by and say hello. I met so many new Black people. When the food was ready, everybody took each other's hands around the room and Alex would say a prayer. It was beautiful. I remember feeling a deep sense of belonging and kinship. Being amongst the Black community there had a profound effect on me. Once the food was done, the boys would talk late into the night about the realities of life in America, how they still had to fight and be strong. We had some really deep conversations.

Eight shows a week in the theatre is tough, especially if you're out at night. Vanessa had insisted Antony be carried dead on stage and remain there till the end of the play so she could die with him which, for me, meant a full twenty-five minutes on my back, playing dead. During the odd matinee I'd fall asleep and catch myself snoring! But it was a great little double to do, Marc Antony and Antony, playing the same character at different points in their lives.

But the end of the run eventually came. I'd been playing opposite Vanessa every night for almost six months, and we had travelled all over the world, but now it was the very last night. I'll never forget it. There was a real charge on stage. Actors can feel when there's a good audience and they pick up on the energy. The place was packed because it was Vanessa's last per-formance, and she was just sublime. I remember lying there dead and opening one eye so I could watch her do the Cleopatra death scene one final time. I glimpsed members of the cast standing in the wings watching her, too. Honestly, it was like she'd been blessed by the man himself. Everyone was in tears and when the lights came up it was all over. I went to my dress-ing room and sat there for ages. I didn't want it to end. I should have been clearing my stuff out to head home back to the 'policemen' and 'lawyers'. That was the plan anyway, but some-thing had happened that night on stage that changed everything. I was in a kind of haze when Vanessa's assistant knocked and said Vanessa wanted to say thanks for the run. I went to her dressing room and we sat and talked and talked. After that we were hardly out of each other's sight for the next six months. Instead of flying home to London as planned, we flew to New

York. Touching down at JFK and heading into town over the Williamsburg Bridge, I could hardly believe my eyes. I'd seen so much of New York in the movies and now here I was. Vanessa had plenty of meetings and was busy most days, so I just walked around the city.

I'd walk all over Broadway, turn into Bleecker and head into Soho. I'd never seen so much style and so many gorgeous people rushing around. It was intoxicating. One evening, we went off to a film premiere to see Liam Neeson in *Michael Collins* and then we headed to dinner afterwards with Liam, Natasha, Johnny Depp and Kate Moss. I kept thinking to myself, *Is this real? Am I having another freak-out?* No, it was all happening.

The following evening we went to a screening of Al Pacino's new documentary *Looking for Richard*, in which he takes huge chunks of Shakespeare out to the people. About twenty of us sat in a small cinema and then a bunch of us went off to eat. I was seated quite close to Pacino and as the evening proceeded we all talked about the film. I remembered a scene where he takes a passage of *The Merchant of Venice* and tries to get a bunch of kids at a school to watch it played out, but the kids weren't really that into it. During a quiet moment after dinner I said:

'I must say, I did enjoy your film but, I think you made a mistake with one of the scenes.'

There was a bit of a hush as Pacino turned to me and said:

'Oh yeah, what mistake was that?'

I said, 'Well, you're trying to get new people into Shakespeare and there's a scene where you have a couple of actors in front of a bunch of schoolkids who are not listening. If you'd had two Black actors doing that same scene, the kids would have been paying attention.'

He looked at me and said, 'My God. You're right. God damn it, you're fuckin right!'

I said, 'I'm only here for a week but I am available for re-shoots if you need me!'

He laughed. It was a fun night.

The next day Vanessa and I went for lunch. She said she was 'meeting a friend' so I didn't give it much thought but when the server showed us to our table, and sitting there waiting was Maya Angelou, my jaw hit the floor and I was actually a bit of a mess. I just about pulled myself together. It was an incredible moment for me. She would slip into poetry mid-conversation if something caught in her mind and just flow.

> *'I fell in love forever,*
> *Twice every year or so.*
> *I wooed them sweetly, was theirs completely,*
> *But they always let me go.*
> *Saying bye now, no need to try now.'*

It was magical. I'll never forget that afternoon.

But my adventure in New York was coming to a close. It had been an experience, but it was time for us to head home to London. I'd been away for quite a while and it was nice to see my friends again. I had developed some strong relationships: Danny and Lui. It was good to be back amongst them.

Workwise, I was back in the cycle of treading water until I was asked to take part in a new season of televised adaptations of Shakespeare's plays. Penny Willcox was directing a version of *Macbeth* in Birmingham, shooting on a council estate and using members of the community in the production and adding professional actors in specific roles. Ray Winstone played Duncan the

King and, my God, the two of us had a laugh. I played Macduff and Andy Tiernan was Banquo. James Frain played the lead. Lovely, lovely actor but fuck, I wanted that role!

Meanwhile, Vanessa was still hoping to stage our production of *Antony and Cleopatra* in New York but it took some time to make it happen, and when it finally did get the green light, I'd been offered Othello at the RSC. My agent really wanted me to take the RSC gig and I spent a whole weekend trying to decide. In the end, I chose to go to New York but it was a tough production. By the time we performed at The Public it had been nearly a full year since Vanessa and I had last performed on stage together. Our relationship was now in a very different place and things were difficult. The team at The Public were fantastic but they didn't get the fiery production we had once created. I take the blame for that, but I couldn't fix what had been broken.

Once after a matinee, I was told I had a visitor who had flown over from London to see me in the show. It turned out to be Sam Mendes. He'd been in the process of mounting *Othello* at the National Theatre with the hot and silky smooth new Black star Adrian Lester, but Adrian had stepped out of the production to take advantage of an opportunity in Hollywood and a starring role in an A-list cast. I liked Sam on the spot, and I agreed to do the show. We ended up with a fantastic production full of first-rate performances with Simon Russell Beale playing Iago and Claire Skinner playing Desdemona. Indira Varma and Colin Teague added superb support and it was a sell-out wherever we took it: Beijing, Shanghai, Tokyo. Mostly what I remember is moving around so much and being the odd one out, especially in Asia, with people staring and pointing.

Flying into New York for the last leg of the tour, I was glad to be where my colour was less of a novelty. I could become just another

Black face and disappear into the crowd as I boarded the coach to take us to our hotel. As we went down Madison Avenue, through the coach window I saw a huge image of Michael Jordan literally covering the whole side of a fifty-storey building. I gasped.

'Look at that!'

But others didn't really get it. It was the biggest image of a Black man I'd ever seen. I found it just so striking, but it was lost on the others.

The show went down well in New York and as I was getting ready for the first night after-show party, I was told there was somebody I didn't know insisting on seeing me. When the gentleman walked in we fell into a really jovial exchange. His name was Robert Thompson and he was a diplomat for the UN. Black, highly intelligent and very funny, I felt at home with him almost straight away. He was impressed with what I'd done and really wanted to know where the hell I'd come from? Who was I, this Black Shakespearean actor turning up out of nowhere? I got on so well with him I invited him to the party. Every now and again someone came up and said how much they'd enjoyed the show and Bob, my new friend, would step back and observe. At one point there was a hush in the room and I saw Bob's eyes widen as he looked over my shoulder. I turned around and walking towards me was the great James Earl Jones. I reached out my hand and he grabbed it.

'Young man, I'm honoured to meet you. That was a fantastic performance. Congratulations.'

We spoke for about five minutes, warmly and genuinely, and then he made his way into the crowd.

Bob, the man I met that night, became a good friend and another of my guardian angels – people who have appeared in my life just at the right time and gone out of their way to encourage me to keep going when I was losing hope.

After *Othello* it was finally time to make some money. I'd been doing theatre for a while now so regular TV work was in order. I got a gig for a show called *The Vice* about a fictional London police station investigating the seedy world of London's sex crimes. It ran for a number of years. Then I got another on a hospital show all about the lives of a group of doctors and nurses. It was sold to me like it was going to be Britain's answer to the American hit *ER* but it ended up a bit like *Coronation Street*. It was fun, though.

I was now filming Monday to Friday in Manchester then driven from the set to my flat in London and picked up Saturday morning to film scenes set in London and driven back on Sunday night to begin filming Monday morning again in Manchester. It was relentless but I was young and enjoyed hitting the clubs on nights back in London, as the lights and the music drowned out all life's cares.

One summer the scene was all about Browns, a cool little spot in Holborn, which was split into different levels. Getting in was the first hurdle, then you had to get upstairs into the red rooms, a far more private area where folks could sit and relax. I met a girl there who I particularly enjoyed talking to. We ended up chatting all night whenever we met there, always catching each other's eye with a nod and a warm smile. It felt good to talk to her. Browns was just the first stop of a very long night back then that would take me and my friends all over London, partying through the night. I remember one night, on the dance floor, when I saw everyone around me was scattering, running and clearing the floor. The music was so good, though, that I just stood still enjoying the moment when my eyes fell on a guy walking towards me with what looked like an Uzi. I froze. I looked the guy right in the eye before he just walked past me. It was as if the whole thing had happened in slow motion. When he was gone, my friend Gary and I looked at each other. We were the only two people left on the dance floor. We just laughed.

Fun as it was, three straight years of this gruelling routine began to wear me down. One night, I was out with Gary and we decided to check out an old spot we used to frequent and, would you believe it, the same girl I used to speak with years before was also there for the first time in ages. I thought it was too much of a coincidence so I asked her out on a date. We began seeing each other and eventually she moved in with me. By now I'd bought my first house and had been rattling around in it alone. It was lovely to have her company and not too long after that our first child arrived.

Lui was delighted with our news. He was desperate to get started on a family of his own. Becoming a father created a monumental shift in my thinking. The focus was no longer me and my career but the family, and how I was going to keep a roof over everyone's head. It was an important change of perspective and it was emotional. I bawled my eyes out during the birth, but I had to snap out of it soon enough because the very next day I had an audition for a big movie, *Blood Diamond*. The role involved playing an African warlord in South Africa and Mozambique and I went along to see the director, Ed Zwick, in his central London office. I was full of the glow of fatherhood. Beaming, I told Ed that I'd just had my first child. We chatted for some time before he said:

'Well, I guess I better see what you got.'

In an instant I switched into a devilish rogue, really enjoying the character's evil intentions. When I finished the two scenes, Ed Zwick just said to me:

'I'll see you later.'

I walked out the door, feeling pretty positive, but it was a solid eight weeks before I heard any news. Financially, things were beginning to get tight. I'd miscalculated the amount of tax Her Majesty would be taking from my earnings and sunk all my money into the purchase of our house. It left me desperately over-stretched and financially vulnerable. It was tempting to take on just anything, but I wanted this role so much that I was prepared to wait for the yes or no. It was a larger-than-life bad-guy part, a chance to finally flex on screen. What a huge relief I felt when I heard I'd got the part.

Soon enough there was a car pulling up to take me to the airport and the limo driver getting out to help with my luggage. On the seat I found a package inside with my name on it containing a new version of the script to read on my journey. It was the first time I'd ever travelled first class and I can tell you, it all felt pretty odd, having just been down the dole office the week before.

I was shown through to the airport lounge, where I put down my bag and helped myself to some of the booze lined up on the counter. There were no staff around, so I helped myself to a second glass of red wine and looked around again to see where I had to pay. Then it hit me: it was free! I got slaughtered and stuffed my face. I couldn't believe the privilege of it all. Eventually I took my seat and saw Halle Berry right nearby. I wanted to say something but I thought better of it and just boarded my flight. Reading the new script, I noticed that there were additional scenes in the rebel camp in which I was commander, but I was only in three of them. I thought, *Hmm, they're missing a trick here, this character is really fun! He should just be around in all of these scenes.* We flew into Durban, South Africa, and I was met by a big, gruff Afrikaner.

'Mr Harewood? My name is Kurt. I'm here to pick you up and take you to your residence', he said in this thick Afrikaner accent.

I slung my bag in the back and jumped in the front like I always did back in those days. Kurt and I travelled through some amazing terrain until finally we reached our location in Port Elizabeth. Costume fittings followed and then weapons training, which was a lot of fun. Before shooting Ed asked to see me. Kurt offered to give me a lift, becoming my unofficial driver for the whole shoot. Ed and I chatted about my audition; he told me that my ability to make him laugh as well as frighten him had swung the day. He hadn't thought of the humour, it had surprised him. I told him I'd read the new script on the plane and that I'd noticed all the new scenes in the rebel camp without my character.

'I should be in those scenes, Ed. I'm not looking for any more cash, I'll happily come in and stand around.'

He laughed and told me I was just trying to make my part bigger! We shook hands and waited for our first day of work together. I remember it well. Ed was doing this wide sweeping shot of the diamond mine that eventually landed on my character delivering a short monologue to all the workers below. I could tell immediately that I didn't have enough lines to cover the camera move Ed was doing, so, as we were setting up, I looked at the prop that had been given to me by the prop master that morning. It had all this pseudo-communist writing on it that sounded really cool so, on the second take, I just said some of these extra lines to cover the camera move. When the camera finally landed on me I said the scripted lines. We did another couple of takes and then Ed walked up to me and said:

'Where are you getting all this extra dialogue from?'

'The props guy gave me a pamphlet written by the real RUF rebel force that swept through Africa. It's the stuff they used to say to people to justify their actions. I thought it sounded good to fill the camera move till the shot found me.'

He nodded and said, 'Okay. Keep going.'

At the end of the day, I was in my trailer getting changed and there was a knock on my door. It was Ed.

He said, 'That thing you said about your character being in all those extra scenes . . . you're absolutely right. I'm going to talk to Leo tonight but stand by for some rewrites.'

Next day, I got a new script that basically made me the de facto bad guy in the movie and I continued to have a ball on set, constantly improvising. On my final day, I packed my things in the car and again jumped in the front. By now Kurt was used to me but he was unusually quiet on the trip to the airport and after a while I looked and noticed he was crying. I said:

'Dude, are you okay?'

He said, 'David. I just have to be honest with you. I didn't take this job to be your driver, it just happened and I got to know you. And . . . I'm a little ashamed of myself because you're the first Black man I have ever truly known and spent time with and I can't believe I've had this view of Black people. I think you know what I'm talkin' about. But you have changed all that. I've got to know you, seen your family, your lovely child, and it's blown my mind what a man you are, and I'm just a bit ashamed.'

It was deep. When I got out at the airport he gave me this massive hug and we said goodbye.

I remember checking in that day and heading through the airport before finally taking my seat in the lounge. When it came to boarding it struck me that after six wonderful weeks in Africa, I was the only Black person in the queue heading home to England. It brought a wry smile as I headed for the first-class seats.

The film did well and picked up a couple of Oscar nominations. Before the Oscars, I travelled out to Los Angeles to see if I could get an agent but nothing was doing. My timing was off. I returned to London where I got a call from the BBC about joining the cast of their new series of *Robin Hood* as Friar Tuck. I ended up creating a sort of Ninja monk version of the friar, and they seemed to like it. A Black Friar Tuck actually made the evening news and was considered fairly controversial. Finally, a television part with a little imagination had come my way. But after a cracking intro, the experience didn't quite turn out how I'd hoped.

As *Robin Hood* was winding up, I was asked to play Nelson Mandela in Johannesburg and I went back to Africa to play the great hero. I felt huge pressure at first but after reading all I could, I decided that rather than being daunted by the legend I would just play the man.

Once again, I waited for something to shift in my career after I returned home but this time I realised there were fresh new faces in town and I had suddenly crossed into stage five of the actors' career: 'Who's David Harewood?' It had all happened surprisingly quickly. I went to see the premier of a new BBC show called *Hustle*, which starred Adrian Lester, my friend, and Marc Warren, Jamie Murray, Robert Glenister and the amazing Robert Vaughn, Hollywood star of work like *The Man From Uncle* and *The Magnificent Seven*. I watched as Adrian starred in this fabulous vehicle, and he was wonderful in it, but I had that feeling that opportunities were already moving away from me.

As I was on the train headed down to Cardiff to do an episode of *Doctor Who*, my now-agent Nicki Van Gelder called to say that a young director had been emailing about a script for a play called *The Mountaintop* about the last night of Martin Luther King's life. Nicki had never heard of this director. He was young and inexperienced, but he very much wanted me to play Martin Luther King. It wasn't something she'd normally put me up for, but because of my breakdown and the delusions of hearing Martin's voice, I was intrigued. I asked her to send me the play to read on the train. I opened the attachment on my phone and read the play from beginning to end in one straight read and decided I was doing it.

It was brilliant, written by Katori Hall, a bright young Black writer from the States who'd struggled to get the play mounted in America because it took an unvarnished look at the legend. It pitted him against a fine young Black waitress who brings him dinner in his hotel room after delivering his famous 'Mountaintop' speech the day before his assassination. It sounds pretty sombre but the play managed to thrill by revealing that the young waitress was, in fact, an angel sent from God to tell Martin that it's his last night on Earth and to be prepared in the morning for death. He refuses to accept his fate, and demands to speak to God on the phone but loses his temper with her, and God (who is a woman) hangs up on him. Eventually he accepts his fate and sees a vision of the future at the end of the play. It's a stunning piece of work and I couldn't wait to get into it.

The up-and-coming young Black actress Lorraine Burroughs was cast as the waitress, and the two of us hit it off. We put together a fifty-five-minute straight, no interval, highly entertaining piece of theatre and staged it above a pub in south London in a small venue called Theatre 503. It was packed every night and brought the house down. I took the same approach that I had with playing Mandela three months before. I played a flawed icon with perfect comedic timing. It became the must-see show in town. The play is highly irreverent and puts the great man's character in some uncomfortable positions, but by the end the audience was sobbing, totally caught up in the magic of the play.

One day when I arrived at the theatre, I received a letter inviting me to come and talk to a group of American students who'd been to see the show the night before, about fifteen students doing a summer course in London. They said they had come to the play knowing the details of the tragic murder of Dr King, and yet within five minutes of the play's opening they were stifling laughter, and struggling to keep a straight face. By the end they'd been on an emotional rollercoaster and had laughed as well as cried. Lui came down to see it, too, and said it was the best thing I'd ever done. He was right. The play transferred to the West End and even won the Olivier Award for best new play. James was nominated in the director section, Lorraine was nominated for Best Supporting Actress. I wasn't amongst the nominees that night, and I've got to be honest, it stung a little. It was lovely that the play won, though. There was talk of a Broadway transfer, but my agent had gently warned me that going to the US with the production was unlikely. Instead, the play finished and I was back where I'd always been, an actor for hire.

I felt as if I was running out of options and time, as a new generation were pushing me further to the side, even though I was still reasonably fit and just in my forties. In contrast, Lui had gained a pound or two. He was a father now, and we often drove up to see him and his new family. After years of sport, his knees were giving him trouble so he decided to get his cartilage operated on. It was meant to be a simple, quick operation, and afterwards he was looking forward to being able to run again. I remember the day because it was my youngest daughter's birthday. By this time I had two beautiful daughters, and my youngest was turning four. We were about to jump in the car and head out for a pizza to celebrate when my phone rang. It was a good friend of Lui's and mine called Graham. We'd known each other since childhood, too.

'Dave. It's Graham. I'm so sorry but I've got some terrible news. Lui's dead.'

I stopped in my tracks, numb. I told my wife and she was brilliant. She took the keys off me and went back into the house to make all the calls and find out what the hell was going on. Apparently, the surgeon had been using a revolutionary new technique that had gone wrong. He'd adapted equipment designed to suck air away from a wound so that instead it would 'blow' cold air into the wound to freeze it and then he used a different technique to remove the cartilage. Unbeknownst to all of us, however, Lui had a condition called osteoporosis or 'porous bones'. The minute the surgeon started blowing air at the wound, it was entering his system. A short time after the operation the oxygen began leaking into his bloodstream, causing an embolism and giving him a massive heart attack. He never woke up again.

I was destroyed. I fell into a deep funk and couldn't get myself out. I didn't cry at first, holding everything in until I lifted his coffin up onto my shoulder and carried him to the hole in the ground. Then tears began streaming down my cheeks and I was proper ugly-face crying. My head cleared after that. I'd lost my best friend and my rock and the one person who'd always believed I was going to make it. I was disorientated for months, unable to understand the new world I was living in. Without Lui, things seemed hopeless and, for a while, I thought I'd never act again.

I had been out of work for six months, my longest stretch of unemployment, when out of the blue I was asked to do a new play at The National called *Welcome to Thebes*. It was the first thing I'd done since Lui had died and I was vulnerable in a way I hadn't experienced before. It suited the production well. When it was over, someone sent me a review that had come out a couple of days before, talking about my performance and saying that if I wasn't given a substantial television or screen role in the UK soon, I'd be off to America. I remember thinking that would never happen.

But Nicki, my British agent, introduced me to an American manager in the hopes of getting me more work there. About two or three weeks later, I got a script called *Homeland* from Vikram, my new US manager. About two weeks later Vikram called me again asking if I'd had a chance to record my audition. I hadn't, but after his encouragement, I picked up my mobile phone, sat on the window ledge, and recorded a half-decent series of four scenes with my wife reading the off lines. It was very basic, so I added a little music on the intro, just to make things interesting and sent it off, thinking they'd never see it.

A couple of weeks later I got a day's work on a James Corden comedy. I'd worked with James many years earlier and now he was throwing me a bone. It was literally a day's work but I was pretty broke, and I hadn't really earned any money for a while so I did my day. When I got home my manager rang telling me that they liked the tape I'd done and that they were getting close to making a decision. I was surprised because I hadn't really given it my best shot. I offered to record my audition again and my manager said it couldn't hurt. I re-recorded my audition with my friend Gary, this time paying a little bit more attention to my accent and the text. A few more days passed with no further news and then one afternoon I got an email from my new agent with just one word on it . . . CONGRATULATIONS. I called him and asked him the news and he told me that I'd just got the role of David Estes in the new Showtime pilot *Homeland*. I was in a state of shock and when I put the phone down. I turned to my wife and said:

'I've got it! I got that show, *Homeland*!'

She looked at me and said, 'David, do you know what day it is today?'

'No?'

She said, 'It's Lui's birthday.'

I teared up. Of all the days. Lui always said I was going to make it and for it to happen on his damn birthday was just too much and a beautiful way for him to say to me, 'I told you so!'

Chapter Twelve

Bright Lights, Big City

I'd never done an American accent before, so I got to work making it sound more natural. I had sixteen days before the start of filming and along with visa and passport paperwork, my hands were full. The time passed really quickly and before I knew it, I was landing in North Carolina and checking into my hotel to start filming.

I remember bumping into Damian Lewis in reception. It was the first time we'd met and he told me that the producers were very excited to have me on the team as they'd struggled to find the actor to play the role. It settled my nerves a little. This was the first big American show I'd done and it was packed full of top-rate actors. I hadn't worked on anything decent in a year and so I felt rusty, meaning that my first couple of days ended up being a little underwhelming.

There's always a sense when you're shooting a pilot that you're not entirely safe, and a bad day at the office can leave you vulnerable to being replaced. I remember sitting in the bar with a British actress who had also flown out to be in the pilot and the pair of us worrying that we were going to be fired as we'd both had rocky first days. In the end I made it but, unfortunately, she was recast and when we shot the series Morena Baccarin took over her role.

I would go to the set some days, even when I wasn't working, just to observe and watch the actors, particularly Claire Danes and Mandy Patinkin. I'd ask the sound guy for a pair of head-phones and just sit and watch how they delivered their lines, how much volume they used, what their process was from rehearsal to action. I was trying to learn as much as I could. Eventually, I found my groove and began hitting some nice notes with Estes. It wasn't a particularly flash role, mostly contained rage, but I enjoyed play-ing opposite Mandy and particularly Claire.

When the show started airing, we knew almost immediately that it was being talked about as a hit. Even before that first season was over we had been nominated for both the Golden Globes and the Emmys. I'd never been to any of those events, but I hastily got myself an outfit and flew to LA for the ceremony. It was such an exciting time, seeing stars of the screen walking around the hotel followed by an entourage of agents, publicists, make-up artist and managers. I could move around pretty easily as nobody really knew who I was.

The hustle and bustle of the actual day was exciting: getting changed early and making our way to the event and the women from the show all looking a million dollars. It was time to preen and pout for the cameras. I was never really that comfortable on the red carpet; it takes some balls to stand there with all those cameras and bulbs flashing. It took me a little while to get settled, but once we were inside and the ceremony had begun, the drink made the evening fly by. Claire won Best Actress but Damian missed out that first year, but when the time came for the big award, Best Show, and *Homeland* was called out, the whole table leaped into the air! Only a year before, I'd been in utter despair but here I was walking past De Niro to get to the stage to stand amongst a group of winners. It was one of the best nights of my life. Later that evening I was heading to the bathroom when I saw Sidney Poitier walking towards me. I shot my hand out and told him what a legend he was. I think he was a little overwhelmed by it, but I just couldn't miss the opportunity.

After a very long and frustrating career in England, I'd finally made it to America, where I'd always thought I might be able to thrive.

Even with professional success and making a name for myself in the States, though, there was something missing. I'd been living in LA for two years and it meant long spells away from my family. We knew there was no alternative if we were to survive financially. I would have rather been working at home, but I couldn't find the roles I wanted in the UK. However, it seemed I wasn't meant to say so. After a BAFTA screening of *Homeland* to an invited audience of TV folk and press, Damian Lewis and I took to the stage to field questions about the show. Towards the end of the Q&A I was asked by a journalist what advice I would give to young Black British actors in England and I said:

'Well, I had to leave, so I'd probably say when they're ready they should get themselves off to the airport to do the same because they're not going to find the same kind of opportunities in the UK as you do in America. Those opportunities don't really exist there.'

The next day the headlines read:

David Harewood says British TV is racist.
I HAD TO LEAVE! Harewood slams racist TV bosses.

It was an uncomfortable couple of days. I wasn't saying anything particularly scandalous, but once again by raising the issue of the lack of opportunities for Black actors, the press had warped my words into some kind of chest-thumping cry for revolution. Talking about race in England really seems to set people off.

I felt free to speak my mind because I knew I had a second season of *Homeland* to shoot and my American career was up and running. I no longer felt restrained in what I said. I knew within a month I'd be living a completely different life and none of this would mean a thing. In a heartbeat, I'd be riding my motorbike through the hills of Topanga Canyon before breaking left onto the Pacific Coast Highway and heading home to West Hollywood. It was like having a foot in two completely different realities. I can remember going to auditions back in the day in England, waiting outside, maybe seeing another actor walk out potentially up for the same role, or making my way through the corridors of Television House for a casting. It was always an odd experience and I felt a little out of place. But when I got to LA, I immediately noticed at my very first audition having to sign in on entry, and on the top of the sheet I was signing in bold print it stated:

PLEASE SEND MORE ACTORS OF COLOR. THESE ROLES ARE OPEN TO ALL ETHNICITIES.

When I went to the next audition it said the same thing again in bold print on the top and I realised I could do anything here. With time, patience and a bit of luck, I could really make something happen. But true satisfaction in Los Angeles is a precious thing. Although there are some who find joy in the city, I wasn't at ease. That familiar feeling came echoing back through me:

Maybe I don't belong here?

It's a feeling that seems to have been with me forever. It's a sense of ghosting through my life. I'm not entirely at home when in England, but then I also feel a sense of emptiness when away and the cycle begins and, once again, I yearn for home. Round and round, split across two countries. Through all of this I never even stopped to think what the impact of this way of life might be on me, away from my family and support systems.

In between seasons, I returned to London. There wasn't really any work around, but I didn't mind because I knew more work was waiting for me in the States. When I returned to the set, I'd got my confidence back and was looking forward to getting into my character's shoes. But early in the season I played a scene with Mandy Patinkin and as we were working through it, I realised that my character was in a far more vulnerable position than I had previously thought. It was just a line that Mandy said that made me think, *Hmm, that's a hint of danger to come.* It was probably my old Spidey-senses kicking back in.

Once again, we were nominated for both major television awards and flew to LA to attend the event. I was more relaxed this time and enjoyed all the press, deciding to not take it so seriously. It worked and I had fun on the carpet. But when we got inside, and as the evening unfolded and all the executives said 'Hello' and filtered by, I began to get an odd feeling. I couldn't quite put my finger on it. I went back to my hotel thinking something was off.

The next morning, I headed for the airport to fly back to North Carolina, distracted but trying not to overthink it. I put some tunes on and attempted to enjoy the flight. When we touched down in Charlotte, my phone started buzzing and there were a couple of messages. The first was from the producer asking if I was still in LA and the second from his assistant asking me to call the office when I had the opportunity. I called when I got back to my apartment and was finally on the phone with the top man. He'd never called me before so I was kind of expecting something and when we spoke, he finally dropped the news on me.

'David, there's no easy way to say this but, David Estes is not going to make it into season three. He's gonna die at the end of the finale.'

'Okay, can I ask was it anything to do with my work? Is that why I'm going?'

'No, not at all. We all love you and what you're doing. The studio asked for a major character to be cut and no matter how we slice it, the only one that'll be impactful is Estes. We love you, man, it's just how it all shook out.'

I was gutted. After putting the phone down, I sat there for ten minutes. I didn't want to go back to waiting for handouts in the UK. I was afraid the good times were over. I called my agents and then decided to write all seven producers an email, just saying 'thank you' for the experience, telling them they had no idea what getting that gig had done for me. It felt good to send the note. Although it was the end of the road for 'Estes', it wasn't for me.

Some months later I headed to LA for 'pilot season', a seven-week period where most networks cast their new slate of written shows or pilots. I was aware of the cattle-call nature of some American castings. *Blood Diamond* had been my very first audition in LA and I saw first-hand how you could be one of thirty guys waiting to audition for the same part, everyone there at the same time! Unsettling stuff. But after *Homeland*, things were different. It was all one-on-one meetings and there wasn't an audition as such. Most, if not all, of the people I was meeting had watched the finale of *Homeland*, the biggest finale of the year! All of them kept asking me the same question:

'Why did they kill you off?'

I think I was getting all these meetings because people wanted to talk to me about the show's decision to kill me! Honestly, getting blown up in that show might have been the best thing that could have happened. After that I made so many new contacts and a multitude of new doors opened.

Another TV show followed, but I was itching to do another film. An opportunity came up to go to Memphis to shoot a film, *Free in Deed*. The script was so demanding that it frightened me, but that's exactly why I decided to go for it. The director, Jake Mahaffy, was a risk-taker known for using non-actors in his projects. He'd become obsessed with the story of a Pentecostal minister who had accidently killed a child whilst performing a 'healing' sermon. It was powerful material and he wanted me for the lead role.

When I signed up to the film, I was based in New York playing the Fairy King Oberon in Julie Taymor's gorgeous production of *A Midsummer Night's Dream*. I had to do my preparation remotely by catching up with Jake on video calls. After the play's run finished, I flew to Memphis and found myself immersed in the most extraordinary community of people. True to form, Jake had persuaded a woman running a local Black church, Prophetess Libra, to let us film her and the congregation comprised of former prostitutes, crack-heads, ex-cons. They all had a story, all were passionately into the spirit, and singing, praising, stomping and charging around the room whilst women fainted and lay on the floor. I was blown away. The singing and the music, complete with organ and drums, were extraordinary, too. As far as the Prophetess was concerned everybody was there for church. She didn't care about the cameras. For her, it was a seventeen-day church service that we would film around.

Memphis was the city where Martin Luther King was assassinated and the Lorraine Motel was not far from where I was staying.

The Black icon had been echoing through my life since my very first stage role and had even spoken to me in my psychotic state, and now here I was standing on the balcony outside of the room where he died with the sound of Mahalia Jackson drifting in from the speakers nearby.

The first two days of the shoot were frantic, filming scripted and non-scripted scenes, and on the third day I came to work ready for action, expecting to be shown to my dressing room, but the assistant paused and asked me to wait. I slung my bag down and wandered over to wardrobe to ask what I was wearing that day and the wardrobe lady said:

'Erm, I've actually been told not to put anything out for you today.'

'I'm sorry?'

'Jake called me last night and just told me to hold off with costumes this morning, so maybe you need to speak to Jake?'

'Okay.'

I suddenly thought . . . *I'm being fired! No dressing room? No costume? I'm gone!* I prepared myself for the news and just as I did, the director Jake walked in. He was clearly distressed, and I really felt for him, so I said:

'Dude. Listen, I think I understand—'

'No, no, let me just get my shit together. So, I watched all of the stuff we've been shooting over the last couple of days last night with the producer . . . and we both agreed, it's not working.'

He was literally on the brink of tears. So I said:

'Listen, if I'm out of here, Jake, all's good man.'

'No. No. It's not you! It's the character! The character I envisioned just doesn't work. I've been thinking too much about the actual guy, the real guy, and that's who you're playing, but somehow it's just not working in the film, man.'

178

'So what do you want to do?'

And he looked at me and said pleadingly, 'Have you got anything else? Could you ... come up with a totally different character?'

'How long have I got?'

He looked at his watch and said, 'Thirty-five minutes.'

My mind switched from anxiety to attention as I jumped up and went to wardrobe to pick out a completely new look. Once I was happy, I went to make-up for further changes. When I had his outer appearance down, I completely threw away everything I'd been thinking over the eight weeks of research. I even threw away the script, deciding to try to find lines of dialogues that felt in keeping with my character. In fact, I didn't look at my lines again for the rest of the film. After the first take that afternoon Jake said:

'That's it. That! Just whatever you're doing now, keep doing it.'

I stayed in this odd state throughout the film, channelling the character without looking at the script and just reacting to whatever situation Jake put me in.

Free in Deed had been my first ever lead film role, and I was blown away to be nominated for Best Actor in the Independent Spirit Awards. I soaked up the atmosphere of the whole awards weekend, attending all the parties. Mahershala Ali was nominated for best supporting actor in *Moonlight* and when I saw him the night before the ceremony, I thought I'd reach out and say 'respect'. I was surprised to find he knew exactly who I was. He told me that years ago he was doing an English accent in a project, and he'd studied some of my earlier work for it. I had to laugh about that.

I knew I wouldn't win the award on the day, but it felt great to be nominated amongst the brightest and the best. On the day of the big event, I looked to my right and saw one of my heroes,

Samuel L. Jackson. I instantly went to introduce myself and maybe even blag a selfie. But as I got out of my chair to walk towards him, he looked at me and said:

'Mr Harewood! We meet at last!'

I nearly fell over. It hit me then that he'd actually taken over the role of Martin Luther King in the Broadway production of *The Mountaintop* and had more than likely seen me in it or knew who I was from that. It was a fabulous day.

My next gig was shooting a new pilot for CBS called *Supergirl*, a DC Comics property in which I was cast as Hank Henshaw, head of the Department of Extranormal Operations. It was a popular, bubble-gum type of show, and I thought it had a good chance of running for a while. No sooner had I agreed to do it than my agent let me know about a BBC project called *The Night Manager*, based on a John le Carré novel. I was already filming by then, so I had to let the role go but two days later they said they could move the schedule to make it work. It would mean leaving the US the same night as the *Supergirl* pilot stopped filming. There wasn't actually a completed script at the time so when the pilot ended at one o'clock in the morning, I went straight from the studio to the airport. I was then picked up from Heathrow and taken directly to the set of *The Night Manager* to start filming. I hadn't even read the script! But I quickly settled in and had a giggle with Olivia Colman.

Before heading back to LA, I played Walter Sisulu in a Mandela project with Laurence Fishburne playing the title role and Orlando Jones playing Oliver Tambo. I had a wonderful time working with the cast, Fishburne in particular. Many years ago, in my wild clubbing days, I'd taken Laurence around the West End and shown him a few of the hot London spots and now here we were, years later, actually working together. *Supergirl* was picked up to series whilst we were filming and at one point, he could tell I was wavering about whether or not to do the job and told me to do it.

'Get a good run of work in America under your belt. Make some money, keep your face out there,' he said.

I listened to his advice. And I'm damn glad I did. I've had a wonderful experience for the last six years, and I've even been given the opportunity to direct a number of episodes too.

The acceleration in the range, scope and complexity of characters that have come to me from America over the last decade has been a welcome change from the narrow, secondary roles I once had to audition for in the UK.

Every now and again I think about just where I started, broken and smashed by a bout of psychosis that nearly derailed my whole life. My illness took me out of the acting game for a while, but it didn't stop me getting work in the long run. If anything, my experience gave me more to draw on as an artist. And when things got tough, as they can in this profession, I relied on the resilience and strength I cultivated whilst ill to get me through. In fact, I'd say that the illness has shaken some of the bullshit from me. The desire for fame and recognition left me long ago, and it may sound like a cliché, but I can say, hand on heart, that it's the work that's most important. Hopefully now I can take advantage of all those years of struggle and find fulfilment in the UK and further afield with the types of roles I used to desperately seek. It's been a long old road, but I think I'm finally ready for my close-up.

Chapter Thirteen

On the Other Side of the Storm

When I look back and consider the path I've chosen, I can see the seeds of who I am today right there back in Birmingham, in front of the television with my family, sitting in the dark with the fire on and maybe a late-night plate of chips freshly cooked on the table. I'm sitting on the sofa next to Mum and Dad, it's Saturday night and it's one of our favourites: *Parkinson*!

The Michael Parkinson show debuted on the BBC in 1971 and aired every Saturday night till 1982. As a kid I must have watched over a hundred episodes. Every week Parkinson would introduce a series of guests, interviewing them about their careers and the things they'd achieved in their lives. Singers and sports stars, celebrities with tales to tell, but I was always fascinated when the actors came on. I was particularly gripped by Richard Burton, Oliver Reed, Robert Mitchum, Shirley MacLaine, Peter Sellers, Peter Ustinov, Jack Lemmon and Walter Matthau. I hung on their every word. They spoke of their journey to fame, discussed the work they'd done; they were stripped of character and yet somehow they appeared authentic, even though you'd seen them in many movies playing 'characters'. They seemed different and captivating and I didn't know why.

I was only nine or ten but something made me lean in whenever they talked about their acting decisions, how they filmed certain scenes. It enthralled me. When I was home alone, I'd pretend I was a guest on the show and sit opposite an empty chair, going through a whole *Parkinson* interview, answering imaginary questions thrown at me by an imaginary Parky. I never chose to be a pop star or sportsman, I was always an actor! Acting spoke to me, almost as if it was pulling me by an invisible thread closer and closer through time till the day I found my way.

I look back now through the prism of all that's happened, and I marvel at my decision to go for it. I don't regret it, but I do wish I'd given it more consideration. At seventeen years old, I had no idea what kind of world I was heading into and no understanding of the psychological toll of the journey I was about to take or of what vulnerabilities it might leave exposed. I was completely unaware of the fault line that runs deep within my psyche between these two parts of my identity;

The English self.

A guest of the country, not rooted, other.

Assimilated.

And:

The Black self.

The two parts only came into focus in relation to racism and the subsequent uncomfortable feelings that came with it. Outside of those experiences, I had yet to create a meaningful relationship with this important part of my identity. And between these two different parts of my psyche, I would eventually lose myself. As I would later read in my medical notes:

4th May 1989, 10.45, Whittington Hospital.
Patient David Harewood.
Very thought-disordered.
Very tense.
Patient believes he is two persons.
Refusing to take medicine as he thinks it will kill him.

Two persons. Two sides. It's almost as if the two different identities were in a battle with each other.

There are memories in my mind of my time on the psychiatric ward that I've never been able to understand. I have only half-formed pictures, flashes of thoughts that I cannot fully make out, but the words in my records complete the picture and I'm able to see things anew.

As a child I heard my mother's voice gently warning me, alerting me to how far down the rabbit hole I was, assimilating and soaking in English culture. I heard it more than once from her but I assuaged her fears and pressed on, keen to explore the world around me, wrapping myself up in the white space, neglecting the history, richness and culture contained within my Black identity. By embarking on my acting career without having that firm grasp on a singular identity, I was building my house on the very fault line that would bring it down. I may have been inspired to be an actor by those I saw on the television, sitting next to Mum and Dad as a young child, but there was one big difference between me and the actors I saw on *Parkinson*. I was Black and I had completely underestimated the significance of that reality.

When I look back and examine what I was saying while experiencing a breakdown, I look for the sense underneath. Just the way we can examine dreams, it's possible to interpret the things I was saying as coming from somewhere deep within my subconscious. I was expressing issues that needed attention, conflicts that needed to play out.

I'm fortunate to have met some amazing people working on my documentary and psychiatrist Dr Erin Turner was the first person in thirty years to actually explain psychosis to me. She has remained a close friend since filming ended, and it's been enormously helpful to have her experienced voice on hand to talk with. She looked over my records and has noted several things that speak to the level of care I received during my stay, particularly the overmedication (both in terms of high doses and frequency) of these old-school antipsychotic drugs, which are heavy and no longer in use. The meds were once known as a 'liquid cosh', something to keep patients sedated and pliant. Erin's helped me learn more about psychosis and understand what I went through as I dig deeper on this, layer after layer, with the picture becoming clearer all the time. I'm finally putting the pieces together from a place of strength.

Something about being an actor actually worked in my favour during my time on the psych ward. There were often odd moments of lucidity during the medicated madness when I'd realise just where I was and how much trouble I was in. I'd focus as if I were doing an acting exercise, concentrating on the details of my situation:

I'm in a brown armchair, the type your nan might sit on. I know all the doors are locked and I can't get out. I can't move anyway. So tired. Other people around me that I do not recognise are wearing pyjamas and shifting oddly. Can't move my hands. Skin really dry. Thirsty. Okay, I'm in trouble here . . . obviously. Watch people's behaviour and see if I note any patterns in their movement. There must be meaning to their idiosyncratic thrusts?

Then I'd fall sleep, and find myself awake somehow in another part of the hospital in the dark.

Must be night time and I hear something, a commotion out-side, a loud voice, another patient, shouting, and something getting closer. I recognise it, it's Shakespeare!

In my confused and tired state I would smile to myself, taking comfort from it, making me feel I wasn't alone.

At about two o'clock in the afternoon on the fifth day of my hospital stay I woke up in a sunlit room and there was a man sitting at the foot of my bed. His gentle face was bathed in the most glorious light. It took me a second to focus, but finally I acknowledged his presence and slowly sat up in the bed. He looked at me and in this beautiful Irish accent said:

'Hello there, David. My name's Gabriel.'

For a split second I thought he was the fucking Archangel Gabriel and my eyes widened!

'No. No. Not that one! Sorry, David, I'm a nurse.'

We actually chuckled about it. We talked for a while and then other people came into the room asking me questions.

8th May 1989, Whittington Hospital.
Has made progress over the weekend.
No longer deluded.
Does not remember delusions.

'That was strange, wasn't it? I feel better. Better than I have done for some time. I think that I lost all my bearings. It's very strange and I find it difficult to cope with.'

No psychotic feelings.
No mood disturbance.
Calm and rational.

I had weathered the storm and got myself to the other side of the madness, pushed myself through the experience and emerged from the other end.

Reading the medical notes revealed how powerless I felt in hospital. One detail really upset me. Flicking through my medical records, I see something that stops me hard. The reports says I was incontinent several times during interviews. Right up until I was ten or eleven, I tended to wet the bed and it meant that I was never able to go on overnight trips at school, something that always irked me. I have vague memories of my mother waking me in the middle of the night to change my bed, standing half asleep in the dark as the light from the corridor shone through the open door. She was used to the routine, so it was pretty automatic. After re-making the bed, she'd give me a hug and I'd climb into the now dry sheets and fall heavily back to sleep.

The mention of incontinence connected to another memory, one I've long struggled to place. It involved a brief bout of uncontrollable incontinence, a fleeting memory of pissing out of a window. All these years whenever it's drifted into my consciousness, I've thought:

What is that?

Just a brief moment, a flash of a memory.

This detail stops me in my tracks:

5th May 1989, Whittington Hospital.
Patient: David Harewood.
Slightly hostile during interview.
Bizarre gestures. Holding his arms up in the air.
Was incontinent of urine during interview.

Bang. The same memory flashes before me again but this time more complete. That's where that memory had come from, all those years ago when I was in that hospital for five days.

I'm in an interview.

Three doctors asking me questions.

Need to get outside.

Outside.

Then I just get up and piss out of the window.

Fuck. That's what that memory is.

I was extremely ill. I've never given as much time to thinking about those five days before. Now, having the records in my hands has allowed me to connect deeply with what was happening. It has filled in a lot of holes and offered a fresh perspective. Of course, I wish I hadn't had to go through that but I'm not sure I'd be who I am if it wasn't for my experience. In a way my breakdown opened my eyes and helped me wrestle with some hard truths.

Before I had embarked on my journey into the acting profession I genuinely didn't think my race would be such a defining issue, but after my breakdown I had a whole new understanding of things. I understood the white space very differently and no longer had any illusions that it was a place in which I would thrive.

Growing up as a Black child, I'd had a healthy fear of the world around me, my Spidey-senses keeping me safe when out and about in the real world. Whenever I did encounter racism, though, it stirred uncomfortable feelings within me. I never knew what to do with those feelings and had never talked to anyone about them. I internalised all of it. There's a real possibility that I turned to clowning and acting, the world of make-believe, to cover those uncomfortable feelings and the questions they threw up within me. Prior to my breakdown I'd simply shut down all internal dialogue about the realities related to my race and then drama school kept me in a protective bubble, shielded me from the politics of the outside world. Within that bubble I could do anything, play anybody. Be ANYTHING! I'd fallen for that fantasy. But in the real world things weren't quite so simple and my psychosis blew the pretence away and ripped the rose-tinted filters from my eyes. I finally came to terms with a far more hostile environment, one in which I will always be othered, limited by the imagination and presumption of some.

If the white space couldn't see it, I wouldn't be it. After my time in the hospital, it all became clearer. I found work with some of the most talented Black actors in the country who wrote, produced and performed in all their own work, sold out venues up and down the country, yet they went unseen by the gatekeepers of the industry; the grey suits of the TV world couldn't see their value. I watched as over time the group drifted apart and I could not but think of the waste. With a little investment and support, they could have produced something uniquely brilliant. Was there any room for Black talent in the white space? I felt I had no value, no currency in the country and it's something I'd have to work hard over the coming years to combat.

My psychosis had revealed a truth that had gone unnoticed before, one that made my English self now feel played, bamboozled, almost embarrassed to admit. He'd been so deep in the white space that he had not seen this truth. How could I have missed it? Meanwhile, my Black self was simply learning more each day, getting comfortable and rearranging the furniture in my mind. I realised I no longer needed my Spidey-senses to alert me to impending dangers; I just had to open my eyes. England would be a particularly difficult place to find success as a Black actor. I could see that much more plainly now.

I remember around this time getting into a bit of to and fro with someone in the industry about this. Marianne Jean-Baptiste, a wonderfully talented Black British actress, had been nominated for an Oscar for her role in Mike Leigh's 1996 film *Secrets & Lies* and we were all buzzing about her success. However, a couple of weeks or so after the ceremony a plane full of young talent was flown to LA to help promote the British film industry and to our shock Marianne was not on the plane. She hadn't even been asked to go. I remember complaining to a powerful agent that she was one of the best! My concerns were dismissed out of hand. I wasn't happy about it. Marianne actually appeared on the BBC's flagship current affairs programme *Newsnight* one evening to discuss the issue and I remember being very uncomfortable watching her have to defend her position in the face of some rather aggressive questioning. The memory stuck with me and it was no surprise to me to learn that Marianne moved to LA shortly after.

That was a turning point for me. When it came to the subject of race in interviews, I was no longer afraid to speak my mind. Over the years this would often put me in the crosshairs of the outraged, that I had the temerity to suggest that there might be something amiss. It got me a reputation for speaking out, which could be extremely difficult. I found that it was pretty much impossible to make nuanced points on race and discrimination in England as most commentators seemed unable to accept that discrimination existed at all. I found the level of denial so profound that it appeared as though *I* was the problem by being 'ungrateful' and by 'rocking the boat'. I made the mistake of once checking the comments section after I'd read an interview that actually sounded quite reasonable only to find it hadn't quite resonated . . .

'He should piss off back to where he came from. Ungrateful little bastard.'

'If it weren't for white people, he wouldn't have a career.'

And you think, *My God, what is the point?* Perhaps that unsettled sense that maybe I really don't belong here stems from hearing sentiments such as these over the years. I do my best not to listen, but I can't help finding it all a little depressing. It's poisonous. Just like Iago pouring pestilence in your ear, it pollutes and ruins your day and it takes a strong mind to defend against it.

Years ago, we all predicted a time when British Black actors would no longer be content with the crumbs thrown down from the men in grey suits in England and would instead be feeding on much more nourishing meals across the pond. And funnily enough, years later on a quick trip home to London during the filming of *Homeland*, I was heading into town on the Tube one afternoon when I happened to pick up a discarded copy of the *Evening Standard*. Flicking through the pages, I stumbled across the headline:

Where have all our Black actors gone?

I chuckled. It went on to name a whole slew of young Black British talent either working in or moving to America, and I think I even got a mention myself! It was just something that even back then I thought was inevitable. I may have been one of the first, but I knew I wouldn't be the last.

Chapter Fourteen

The Large Black Man

People cautioned me about looking further into my break-down, warning it could bring up long-buried pain best left to rest. Although I listened to their concerns, the journey into my past proved important, necessary work. I'm finally putting the broken pieces of my identity back together again and understanding my breakdown from a whole new perspective. Working on the project was the first time I'd stopped to consider how race, identity and the decision to become an actor had all played a part in my undoing.

During filming, I was handed an envelope containing my medical records from the Whittington Psychiatric Hospital, where they had been kept on file all these years. The notes were in my possession for over a year before I had the courage to look at them because, to be honest, they make for uncomfortable reading. The envelope contained all the reports and interviews I did with psychiatrists, what drugs I was given, what dosages, and even reports on my behaviour during my stay at the hospital. The records provide a fascinating account of my shattered, deeply deluded and highly disturbed younger self. It's been tough to sit with what happened during my hospitalisation, in particular some of the things I said.

2.15 p.m., April 1989, Whittington Hospital.
Patient: David Harewood.
Attempted to talk to him in a room on his own.
(6 policemen outside door + 1 male nurse)
Very hostile.
Shouting . . . 'I have to save the boy.'
Believes he has merged hearts with a young Black boy.

That is what I was screaming just before they rushed into the room and restrained me. I remember being confused and terrified. First I had completely lost control of my mind and now my body was under assault. They performed a 'rapid tranquillisation', which was as terrible as it sounds. Whilst I lay there, just trying to stay alive on the floor with seven people holding me down, the drugs slowly started pulsing through my body. I was held down for about two hours until finally I stopped resisting. I was really out of it, hallucinating and too exhausted to stand up. I thank God that I had friends advocating on my behalf at the hospital otherwise I'm not sure what would have become of me. Had they not been there, making noise and making a nuisance of themselves, I could have found myself on the way to any one of six different hospitals.

11.40 p.m., Whittington Hospital.
Patient: David Harewood.
No Beds!
Tried St Anne's
St Luke's

N. Middx
UCH
St. Pancras
Friern
Islington/Haringey

It's a feature of the often chaotic and unpredictable nature of dealing with patients who are experiencing various forms of mental illness that the availability of beds in secure units on any given night can be a major issue. It wouldn't be unusual for a patient to be driven up to a hundred miles for an available bed. Having lived through the experience, I can only thank fuck that I didn't wake up somewhere strange surrounded by frightened staff who thought I was just a crazy Black man with dry skin and nappy hair, aggressive, dangerous and scary.

In my own records I'm often described as a 'large Black man' and it's also interesting to note the very high doses of drugs I received (Diazepam and haloperidol), both at levels four times the current recommendations. What was the thinking behind these high doses? Were they afraid of me? Was it to control and subdue, as opposed to treat and help? Was it a decision rooted in fear of the 'large Black man'? It's no wonder Black people are so reluctant to seek help with their mental health.

According to the latest NHS figures, Black men in the UK aged between thirty-five and forty-nine are four times more likely than white men to be detained under the Mental Health Act and ten times more likely to be under a Community Treatment Order (CTO). The figures for Black women are also disproportionate: roughly six times more than white women. Consider for a moment how relatively rare incidences of serious mental ill health are in Black men and women of a similar age living in the Caribbean. I don't need anyone to explain that to me. Living in the UK where Black pain is denied, where your concerns aren't listened to, and where your self-worth is so non-existent that it seeps into the very fabric of your being,

Black people are reluctant to seek help because they regularly experience not being heard and they fear they will be overmedicated instead of treated. To voluntarily enter the mental health system as a Black man, especially a British Black man who is 'supposed' to have a stiff upper lip, is to place yourself in an extremely vulnerable position, which could easily exacerbate an already frayed mind. This is why diversity in the mental health services is so important because seeing another face that looks like yours might just be enough to calm a frightened and confused patient and make their experience a little less alarming. A psychiatric ward is a dangerous place to be 'othered' in. Which is probably why, like me, so many Black men only enter the mental health system at a point of crisis rather than seeking help at an earlier stage. Can you imagine waking up in a hospital you don't recognise, surrounded by people who don't know you, full of antipsychotic drugs and only being referred to as the 'large Black man'?

Luckily for me, my friends Nick and Jeremy were with me at the hospital and stood by me at my hour of need. They pleaded and begged the staff not to simply abandon me to the system, and their request was finally granted when a bed became available in a building not far from the Whittington. They bundled me into a wheelchair and, along with a hospital porter, wheeled me out of the hospital, onto the street, and up the road towards the available bed. In fact, the bed already had two people booked into it. God knows what happened to them but I was grateful. I was extremely groggy, tired and heavily medicated on a cocktail of drugs, but through the haze I can just remember overhearing a conversation between the hospital porter and one of my friends:

'Why is he always talking so much?' said the porter.

'He's an actor. They're some of his lines from a play,' came the answer from my friend.

It's difficult for me to think about that night. How, just two years out of drama school, did I end up in a wheelchair, out of my mind, spouting lines from old plays dredged up from my memory and being committed to a mental institution? How did I become so detached from myself? Looking back on it, I believe 'the boy' I had to save was my younger self, that same little boy I used to be. I was merging hearts with him and trying to get back to him. Somewhere in my scrambled mind I felt I had to get back to that boy and reconnect with him. He was the one who started it all, the clown who messed around and dared to dream. *That's* the boy I had to save. But smashed and babbling, immobilised and pumped full of drugs and hitching a ride in my NHS chariot on the way to Crazy Town, I wasn't capable of saving anybody. It's hard to think the little Black boy who so enjoyed clowning around could end up in this situation. How did he get here?

It's a question I had really put to the back of my mind for years. After my psychosis, I tried to just get on with my life but occasionally, out of the blue, I'm reminded of what I went through. Each time it packs a punch. Once, for example, I was playing Othello at the Swan Theatre in Worcester and one night a friend of mine from London travelled down to see the show. After a boozy night catching up, we headed out for breakfast the next morning on the high street when suddenly, out of nowhere, two police cars came screeching to a halt on the pavement and four coppers jumped out and arrested us! We were put in separate cars and driven to a nearby police station and each checked into separate cells. My friend, Paudge, a fiery Irishman, was letting them have it from his cell whilst I quietly sat knowing we hadn't done anything wrong and waiting for them to realise that and let us out. Turns out as we were walking up the high street one of the local shopkeepers thought we were the same two guys who had robbed her shop the week before! A Black kid and a white kid – obviously us, right? That's what we were that morning, criminals apparently, and now we were each in a cell. After about thirty minutes, Paudge was released. He was SO pissed off. Really giving it to the duty officers and demanding to know when I, too, would be released.

'There's an issue with Mr Harewood. If you wanna wait, it's up to you but it may take some time.'

Another officer came into my cell holding a piece of paper and he looked up at me and said:

'Mr Harewood, do you recall an incident in 1989, the third of May, involving you jumping out of a taxi and not paying? You were arrested and set a date to appear in court.'

I instantly knew what he was talking about. It was that terrible night in London and I knew I was in potential trouble, so I told the officer that I'd had a breakdown shortly after that night and I'd completely forgotten about it and that I was an actor in town playing Othello at the local theatre. He said:

'Thing is, Mr Harewood. As you didn't show up for your court appearance, an automatic warrant is issued that should you be arrested, anywhere in the country, you are to be held in custody until the appropriate authorities can collect you.'

My heart sank. The night my world had collapsed had come back to haunt me. I told Paudge to head on home as there really wasn't anything he could do. I asked to make a call and phoned the theatre. It was midday by now but I was already thinking about the show. Even the theatre's lawyers tried their best to get me out to at least do the show! The police were having none of it and eventually I was returned to my cell and the show was cancelled that evening. At about three in the morning a police car from London arrived, and two large coppers walked in to collect me. Apparently on my file it had referred to me being a 'large Black Man' and so they'd sent PC Beefy and his brother down especially for me. I was so tired that I was no trouble at all and after a brief chat with them as the paperwork was being done, they just let me walk out and sit in the back of the car. They didn't even bother to handcuff me. They'd come all the way from London to Worcester to collect me, and told me that nobody wanted the job, that it had been on the board all day but they'd pulled the short straw and had to get it done. We chatted for a bit and they were interested in my acting. I'd done an episode of *The Bill* and they wanted to know all about it, but I wasn't really in the mood. I talked for a bit and crashed out. I'd been incarcerated all day and now I was on my way to London and I just wanted to get the whole thing over and done with.

We arrived at our destination pretty early and I managed to get a couple of hours' sleep on the way before once again finding myself sitting in front of a duty solicitor answering charges related to getting in that cab, but because I didn't appear for my court hearing there were extra charges. I explained the situation to the solicitor, telling him the story of my breakdown and that I'd moved to Birmingham to recover and simply forgot all about it. He totally understood the picture and when it was my time to appear in the dock I remember walking up the stairs of the court and facing the judge in his robes across the room with packed benches all around. When my name was called, I stood and answered, then the solicitor said:

'Your Honour. Mr Harewood is a young and successful actor who studied at the Royal Academy of Dramatic Art. He's currently playing Othello at the Swan Theatre in Worcester where he was arrested on a separate charge, for which he has since been proven completely innocent. However, the court's charges relate to an incident that occurred in 1989 during a period when Mr Harewood was experiencing a mental breakdown after which he was subsequently hospitalised. He has only a brief memory of the incident and, in light of the circumstances, I would ask Your Honour to show leniency, particularly as Mr Harewood is performing tonight after unfortunately being forced to cancel last night's show as a result of being at Your Majesty's pleasure.'

The Judge looked at me and just said:

'Get thee gone!'

There was a chuckle around the court, and I'm sure if I'd have been in a better mood, I'd have laughed myself but I was too tired for levity. It was already 11 a.m. and I had to get back to Worcester to do the show. I nodded to the judge, turned and walked straight out of the court, jumped on a train, popped into my digs for an hour and went straight to the theatre to play Othello.

Chapter Fifteen

Going Public

I was in Soho House, LA, one night when a young Trinidadian girl walked up and introduced herself to me. Her name was Sabina, and she was a stylist from London. After about ten minutes I knew I was going to work with her. She had some great ideas and got me thinking about social media and how to use it in connection with my work. I liked that social media was different from day to day. It seemed harmless fun. I mainly tweeted simple stuff to pass the time and connect with fans.

A couple of years rolled by and the production of *Supergirl* moved to Vancouver, a beautiful city in Canada. I found an apartment overlooking False Creek, just a short walk to the water's edge. Things felt different in Vancouver. There was not such a desire to see and be seen. People in LA are super conscious of their appearance, even when just popping out for a pint of milk. There was no such pressure in Vancouver, and I found the change of scene and speed refreshing.

When I had gaps in my schedule, I would often fly home to spend time with the family, walking the dog, and just trying to be a dad. Going home always gave me a chance to reset, take a breath, catch up with friends and gain a fresh perspective. During one of my trips in 2017, Sabina and I met up at the *GQ* Men of the Year Awards. It was a fun night, and we scheduled a quick debrief before I headed back to Vancouver. During the conversation she mentioned that it was World Mental Health Day and suggested I tweet a supportive message as she knew I had an interest in that area. I thought it was a good idea and headed home to pack my things. Standing in my kitchen hours later, with the cab on the way, I picked up my phone and casually tweeted:

> So, it's #WorldMentalHealthDay today. As someone who had a breakdown and was sectioned in my twenties, I'm here to tell you that there's no shame in talking about it, if you're struggling. I haven't done too bad since! Go easy on yourself today. And get some help if you can.

Almost immediately I could see that the tweet was getting traction but just then the cab arrived. I said the usual 'goodbyes' and hugs and kisses erupted all around the house. I didn't really check my phone again until I was properly on my way to the airport in the cab.

Checking back into my Twitter feed, seeing some of the responses, I found myself responding to people who had also experienced something similar, all commenting on my mental health tweet. I began interacting with many of them and within a short time they were interacting with each other. Right before my eyes, a little self-supporting community of people were communicating in my timeline.

When I arrived at the airport, I put the phone away to pass through security and didn't bother to get it back out of my bag. I headed straight for the BA lounge and the free whisky, a regular move of mine, and settled down to eat some crisps and watch what was on the telly. I think David Lammy was in the Commons making another one of his stand-out speeches. In quick time I was on the plane and sleeping, the whisky doing its job nicely and knocking me out, and after another quick flight I landed in Vancouver. In the cab on the way to my apartment I switched on my Canadian phone to check in on my messages and was slightly shocked to see my mental health tweet had over two million interactions and been liked over thirty thousand times! There were emails, too, from my agent, requests for interviews. I'm sure they hadn't got a clue what all the sudden interest was.

What has he said now?!

I ended up doing a couple of quick interviews and also an article in a newspaper, talking about my breakdown being some wild and crazy adventure that had happened to me thirty years ago. I spoke about it almost as if it had kind of been fun! It had happened so long ago that the memories were faded now, embellished over the years in some kind of psychic mind trick. In truth, I only had glimpses of what had really happened, faint memories. I made the whole experience sound as though it was nothing. I remember writing of the breakdown that there was 'treasure in it', something of benefit, but I didn't say what it was. To be honest, I didn't exactly know. I just knew something about the experience had given me something. The article went out a couple of days later and again it seemed to get a fair bit of positive reaction, but when my old friend Danny happened to read it, he was heard saying:

'That's not how I remember it.'

When a mutual friend told me this a couple of weeks after the article went out, I was puzzled. I thought, could it be that I'd mistaken my mental breakdown experience? Forgotten the facts about what had happened me? I was curious. Over the past couple of years, I'd been lucky enough to present a couple of documentaries. One of my first was on failure in the acting business, for which I interviewed Naomi Harris, Damian Lewis, Brian Cox, Zachary Quinto, Ed Zwick and Olivia Colman about times in their career when they had faced up to failure. It's a great watch, especially for actors, as I reveal that 'failure' is just another part of the business to navigate and that resilience can pay dividends down the line. I also made a documentary on the inequalities in the education system facing young Black Britons called *Will Britain ever have a Black Prime Minister?*. It was a highly topical programme and I very much enjoyed working in the genre, asking questions and mixing my comfort in front of the camera with rich, hot-button issues. Documentaries gave me another vehicle of expression, slightly different from acting, free from the artifice of sets and props.

Away in Vancouver, with time on my hands, I couldn't help thinking that finding out what really happened during my psychotic breakdown would make a great documentary. Obviously I no longer remembered exactly what had happened, and it could be a journey in which I might finally learn the truth about it. I made a few calls and pitched the idea. I was excited, keen to finally uncover the facts, but as filming on *Supergirl* picked up steam and England once again became a far-off memory, the whole project seemed to grow cold. Discussions were being held, but being away, I wasn't privy to them, so I just threw myself back into my work.

After a couple of months, however, I heard the news that the BBC were interested and were in the preliminary stages of trying to put the production together. I was quite buzzed. Wendie Ottewill was brought on as director and I remember the two of us having an early call; she seemed nice and, as we chatted, I pretty much agreed not to ask too many questions going forward and just let myself experience the film in the moment – something I really appreciate about working on non-scripted projects. I trusted myself enough to be able to handle it. We discussed some of the main ideas such as potentially meeting up with my old friends Nick and Jez and Danny and I was instantly on board. I hadn't seen Jez in over twenty-five years and Nick and Danny only very briefly over that time. I was looking forward to catching up with them. What I didn't see was the storm that was coming. As Christmas came and went and *Supergirl* filming finally drew to a close, I found the months away had left me weary, and longing for rest. When I returned to England, that's not what I was about to be getting, not at all.

I have a habit of signing up for a new project before I've actually finished my current one. It always sounds easy at the time and sometimes it is, but not this time. No sooner had I flown home and got my feet in the door than Wendie was looking to start filming. Within a week she came over to my house with a very small crew; cameraman Seb, assistant producer Olivia and Wendie and I spent half a day filming, just a gentle warm-up, the calm before the storm. It went well and everybody seemed like a good fit for the shoot. I liked Wendie's gentle probing questions and as the week drew to a close, I was thinking this might be easier than I'd imagined. The following week, though, things began to get more difficult. It was then that this whole thing pulled me into the abyss.

I was scheduled to meet with Nick and Jez in central London, in the pub we used to drink in as students thirty years ago. When they arrived, I was genuinely delighted to see them. My God, I suddenly realised it had been decades, and we instantly began catching up and laughing together. The team were brilliant and the filming was easy. It felt almost as though the camera wasn't there. As we talked more, it hit me like a thunderbolt: the story I had held loosely in my mind all these years wasn't quite correct. Jez told me that back when it was all happening, they had been out looking for me on the streets, knowing I had a tendency to go walkies. Going walkabout was the first sign of trouble, apparently, but because we were having such a good time catching up, I brushed off my shock and continued chatting. At this point none of us had discussed what had happened when I'd had my breakdown. Of course, we'd met briefly when I recovered, but we'd never really talked in depth about how the experience had affected us personally or what emotional toll psychosis had wrought on me or on them. It was all just unfolding in front of the camera, but not quite in the way I'd expected.

After this mini reunion we made our way outside and piled into a van to continue filming. We were headed to the Whittington Hospital to retrace the steps of the day that I was hospitalised, and as we continued talking and filming both men began to inform me of the truth. I continued to be surprised by the information, which wasn't how I had remembered it at all. I started listening intently. Nick mentioned that I was saying I had three people's brains in my head and that I could potentially kill them if I died. It all sounded very bizarre, but as they carried on talking the memories of the day began slowly coming back to me. I looked out of the window of the van and something about the place seemed familiar, the streets reminding me of that fateful day. The memories started to flood back now and suddenly I became very aware of camera filming me, watching me. This wasn't like acting, there was no character to hide behind, no script to offer structure. This was all about me and I was deeply uncomfortable, aware of the camera's piercing gaze. I tried to jolly along, keep my spirits up, look professional, but it was getting harder and the more I heard from them the more I felt really exposed.

We parked the van and walked in where the old entrance of the hospital used to be and there, Nick and Jeremy explained what had got me through this doorway. I saw Nick get momentarily upset as he described how I was screaming and highly distressed, on my knees, crying out at the top of my voice. I was desperately covering now and drawing on all of my acting skills, surprised at Nick's emotion, before Jeremy completed the story and told me about the emergency rapid sedation, during which several policemen rushed at me and restrained me on the floor. That's when I first realised how much this had also affected others, the people closest to me, and the impact of that realisation hit me hard. This moment was the first time I got emotional in the film, and the first time I remembered just how very ill I'd been.

This episode wasn't the fun little freak-out I'd made it out to be all these years, this was a full-on psychotic breakdown. We paused filming for a while to allow me to catch my breath. I was reeling, all the memories flooding back: being held down, terrified, not understanding what was happening to me, and the overwhelming fear of being institutionalised. Suddenly, I was transported back thirty years to the very moment of utter mental collapse. Wendie asked me to try to explain how I was feeling and I guess my professional senses kicked in. I was here to make a TV programme after all, right? *Get yourself together.* But I was struggling with the emotion, trying to process everything. *Fuck, this actually happened?* I was pretty upset and remembered everything clearly now. The windows of the buildings, gazing at the surrounding rooftops, wishing I was outside sitting on the grass. It was a powerful moment. I'm not going to lie, from that moment on until filming ended, I was terrified. I didn't know what other forgotten memories were going to come and find me.

I couldn't stop thanking both Nick and Jez for what they had done for me – they had literally saved my life. How had I not realised that? I had buried their friendship and their own pain of the moment along with my own. Now I was achingly aware of how much they had gone through in order to help me that day. I felt very guilty that I had not given them space to talk about this until now, thirty years later. My affection for them grew enormously.

Later that day Wendie had arranged for me to collect my medical records from my time on the ward, the idea being that I sit and share some of the info with Nick and Jez. But when I picked up my records and opened the envelope to shoot that sequence, I didn't want to discuss what I saw on the page.

Feels he has merged hearts with a Black boy.

That was too much for me to take. I was getting a glimpse of my younger, crazy self and so I closed the envelope and changed the subject. We ended up not using that sequence. From time to time over the course of the shoot Wendie would sometimes ask me to refer to the notes for filming purposes but I never once read a single word. I was too afraid. I'd put my eyes in soft focus and pretend I was reading through them but, in truth, I wasn't. When filming ended, I put the notes in an envelope that I didn't open again until I started writing this book, nearly two years later. The envelope contained dynamite. I wasn't ready to handle the truths contained in its pages.

I returned home that night feeling I'd made a huge mistake embarking on this project. I was a wreck and struggling psychologically. I tried to hide it, but the pressure of remembering what had happened seemed to be recreating those same thoughts and feelings. I was overthinking. As my mind was beginning to spin, I kept saying to myself:

Get a grip, you are not having another breakdown!

The next day I was scheduled to meet up with another old friend, Danny, and I was scared to hear more damaging information. Luckily, Danny had something very different to say. It was lovely catching up. Although I'd seen him once or twice since I was hospitalised, this was the first time we'd spoken about it in depth, open and honestly. During the interview Danny told me he had been wrapped up in excitement about my thinking at the time, almost as though I'd reached a new understanding of things. He told me it seemed that I appeared to be experiencing something positive. Hearing Danny's perspective really helped me that day. I'm not sure if Danny said it just to make me feel better, but it was reassuring to hear something about my experience that was close to how I remembered it. Danny acknowledged that there were moments of great creativity. At times I had felt that what I was going through was almost spiritual, transformative. It was like getting messages from another realm. Early on in the psychosis, there were periods when I was incredibly high, full of energy and wild ideas. Either way, it was a huge relief to hear him confirm that side of it after what I'd learned the day before. After meeting up with Danny, I just started counting down the days till filming was all over.

The following week we began filming at an Early Intervention Centre in Birmingham helping young kids who'd experienced psychosis recover under the supervision of a specialised team. Erin chatted with me in between set-ups. We'd arrived there hoping some of the kids might want to appear in the film. All of the young people in attendance had recently had experience of psychosis and were in recovery. At first, they weren't paying me too much attention. I sat in on a class Erin was delivering about how psychosis affects people and describing the biological factors at play in the brain throughout a psychotic event. I found myself listening intently. This was more information on psychosis than I'd heard in thirty years; much of it was new to me and I found myself truly engaged. I watched as she presented a masterclass on hallucinations and delusions. Fascinated by what I was hearing, at one point, Erin asked the group a question about hallucinations and I put my hand up and answered. From the corner of the room I heard:

'How would you know?'

'Well, I know because I had psychosis years ago and was sectioned in London. That's why I'm making this film.'

Suddenly the atmosphere in the room changed as all the kids in the class turned to look at me.

'You had psychosis?'

'Yes,' I said.

We began talking amongst each other and I had to apologise to Erin for hijacking her class, but she was willing to let the kids open up and talk to me with the cameras rolling. It was a special moment as they began to tell me of their own experiences. I realised that that was the first time I'd sat in a room with other people who had been through a similar experience. Young people, boys and girls, Black and white, all in recovery from a psychotic event. I felt blessed to be amongst them. My own recovery thirty years before had been almost entirely a solo affair, and now I could look around and see the faces of young people who had also lost touch, momentarily, with reality.

After the class, a couple of the kids expressed an interest in talking further about their experiences. In the end these contributors became an integral part of the programme. In many ways they kept me going, inspiring me with their courage and strength to push on when I was feeling low and tired. Unfortunately, I'd been spending an increasing number of my filming days in Birmingham and it was getting under my skin. Finally, here I was at home in England. Why the hell was I staying in a hotel? Why wasn't I at home with my family, resting? I started giving myself a hard time.

During the day, though, things were fine. I was filming with a wonderful psychiatrist, Rowena Jones. She worked out of a new hospital in town and she was introducing me to the more clinical side of psychosis. Again, I was fascinated to be learning so much about the condition. I was even able to interview a young lady who was, at that moment, in a psychotic state. It was extraordinary.

At one point Rowena took a brief look at my medical records. The sequence we had in mind was that she would read some of the notes and perhaps be able to shed some light on what might have been going on. I was apprehensive about shooting this, worried that having someone explain the situation might tip me over the edge. I was nervous but in the end Rowena's calm and studious manner put me at ease as she cast her eye over my secrets.

'You knew someone who was going to buy a wine bar where you would be able to pluck a guitar out of the grass and play it.'

'And what's this, you have to "save the boy"? Who do you think the boy is?'

I'd not heard any of that before shooting. I recognised the reference to the wine bar and Colin, but when it came to 'the boy' I was stumped for a moment before realising and saying:

'I think it's me.'

That was the first time I thought that the envelope's secrets might contain more answers than just painful secrets. But we'd moved on by then. Filming meant that sometimes we were out late at night, waiting for a blue-light call: an emergency that we could latch on to and follow to film. It meant hours of waiting around late into the night. All the officers and people I was meeting deeply impressed me. They formed the Street Triage Team, making a change in how mental health cases were dealt with. The unit was created after a number of mentally ill people had been restrained and this had resulted in their death. A tipping point had been reached and too many people, particularly Black men, were dying whilst in restraint.

The Triage Team were taking a different approach and I found their system encouraging. They'd had to volunteer for the unit. It was their chosen way of making a difference. Usually nothing happened and it was beginning to get a little tiresome. After a couple of days I blagged it so that I could wait in my hotel instead. I was only round the corner, so if it came to it, I'd just drive over. But soon enough I was finding the confined space of my hotel room suffocating and I began to hit the minibar. I wasn't really sleeping well either, and I was starting to worry a little. Although production had provided me with a host of numbers and support aids throughout filming, I was still finding it tough. Before filming I'd thought I was in a much better place with my mental health history than I actually turned out to be. Trying to process everything as well as present the programme was beginning to take its toll.

Filming coincided with the bi-annual charity football match Soccer Aid. I'd agreed to participate in this huge, televised live football match sponsored by UNICEF and played between an England team and a World team made up of former professional footballers and celebrities. They must have heard about my goal-keeping skills because I found myself in goal. I really enjoyed it and played well and even saved a couple of penalties! The match gave me the chance to get away from all the trauma of filming and have a laugh. I had such a great time meeting some of my footballing heroes and cracking up with Paddy McGuinness and John Bishop.

The morning before the game I was sitting at breakfast and I was joined by one of the team doctors. We got chatting about *Homeland*, and he asked me what I was doing now. I told him about the documentary and told him how tough I was finding it. He encouraged me, saying it was an important thing to be talking about and that it would help a lot of people. He told me that he, too, had had some kind of breakdown as a medical student many years ago and had had to take a little time out to get himself together. I'm always amazed how many people have experienced bouts of serious mental distress – successful people, professional people. It really is more common than you might think.

I played the game in Manchester, travelled back to London to pick up my car and then drove up to Birmingham to interview one of the contributors, a young girl from the class. She was the same one who had asked me:

'How would you know?'

She'd agreed to speak to me on camera about her experience, but by the time I arrived back in Birmingham, I was exhausted. I remember taking a moment in the car to get my head together and just breathe. I sat in silence in the car park for ten minutes before walking in. In the end, we had the most amazing chat. She was so honest and brave that she took away my own anxieties simply by being herself. She became emotional at one point and I was right there with her. I told her how she was inspiring me by being so open.

When the interview was over, I walked outside and told Wendie I was close to done, unsure of how much more I could do. I headed back to my hotel to crash but found that I still couldn't sleep. I was wired, running through everything that had been going on, thinking about what I'd been learning. My mind was spinning. I was getting agitated, sitting up in bed, turning on the lights watching TV – anything to distract myself and enable me to sleep, but it wasn't working. At about four o'clock in the morning I made the fatal mistake of checking my Twitter feed and there under a tabloid header banner was:

ENGLAND GOALKEEPER HERO DAVID HAREWOOD IN PSYCHO DRAMA!

I thought, *What the fuck is this?*

After I first came out about my breakdown, I had given one very sensitively handled interview. I said what I did about my breakdown with a broadsheet newspaper specifically for Mental Health Awareness week, but in the end the piece wasn't used. However, now that I'd played well in the Soccer Aid match, some sub-editor thought it would be a scoop and a bit of fun to take that same interview and hack it to pieces. They wanted to make it sound glib and sensational by running the England goalkeeper and mental breakdown stories together. It really pissed me off. Nobody from the newspaper told me the piece was coming out and it really, really stung. I felt angry that my trauma was being sensationalised in a throwaway article. It felt abusive. I called Wendie and left a message on her phone telling her to call me ASAP. Eventually, she did and came over right away. We sat in the bar as the hotel staff were prepping breakfast and she could tell I was upset. She had to work hard to calm me down and then cancelled filming for the day. We just sat and spoke about the newspaper article and how it had diminished my experience.

I began to realise that my feelings in the moment mirrored some of the feelings I had had thirty years ago. Reading upsetting things about myself in a newspaper, knowing that I had been treated with a total lack of care when the piece was written, compounded by a sense of isolation had a drastic impact on my mental well-being. It reminded me of the old reviews I used to get and how easily they'd dismissed me and devalued my sense of worth. Wendie suggested we include these feelings in the programme. A couple of days later when we returned to London, I spoke with a Black clinical psychologist, Chanel Myrie, about how racism and the environment can impact Black mental health. It was illuminating. I felt so much better knowing my frustrations were real and valid and that for a Black person, living in the white space can be very difficult.

When I really stopped to think about it, I was surprised I didn't have psychological issues earlier. Drama school can be a challenging experience for many young actors as one's identity inevitably comes under pressure. This was confirmed to me when two weeks after my documentary aired, I received a message from a tutor at a drama school in London asking me if I could talk to one of her students. He was a young Black lad who had experienced a breakdown similar to mine and was struggling to find a way back. I wanted to be there for him but I was so battered in the days after the doc aired, I didn't really have the strength at that time so I offered other resources. I would be really interested to know the number of actors making their way through drama school who have experienced some kind of psychosis and struggled with their identity.

Psychosis requires early intervention and professional help. Whilst some choose to live with mild conditions as best they can, it can be dangerous. If left untreated, a person can quickly spiral out of control, as my father did, and then require hospitalisation. There's a fear that descends when you realise an ambulance is there to take you away. I didn't see it first-hand with my father but I had the opportunity to witness emergency interventions whilst filming the documentary. I went out on blue-light runs with the West Midlands Triage team and saw mental health checks and detentions from a different perspective.

As I mentioned previously, this team had been set up as a result of the many deaths that were occurring during detentions, particularly those of Black men. The idea was to decriminalise the detention process and create a specific team, including a mental health nurse, security detail and a nurse practitioner, to attend all calls with the necessary skill sets and a mental health dimension, taking the burden off the police. Prior to the creation of the unit it was the police who dealt with public disturbances, which often led to tragedy. This new unit had a different approach. I was impressed with how they went about their business.

We were out on a call one afternoon, racing through the streets at high speed to see a man refusing to go into his house. His friend had called the authorities after being unable to get through to his old friend. We were filming the whole process so I was aware of the camera but as we pulled up to the scene there was an old West Indian guy who looked just like my father standing outside the front of the house. I was genuinely caught a little short. He was around the same age my dad was just before he died, and his hair was the same. Even the skin on his hands reminded me of my father's, old and leathery from years of toil. I looked inside the house to see what the situation was and no sooner had I entered than I was overwhelmed with the state and smell of the place. There was rubbish everywhere, each surface covered with discarded and half-opened ready meals and empty pill packets with all different kinds of tablets that looked like they'd been spat out. Mould grew aggressively all over the cooker and when I checked out the fridge I nearly threw up. I began to get a bad feeling, particularly after I spotted the carers' notes that had been scribbled in a notepad and left under a pile of crap. It hit me that this old guy was supposed to be being looked after and cared for, but he had just been left alone to take care of himself. His family was nowhere to be seen and he was overwhelmed by everything.

I walked out, composed myself and then tried to talk to the man. Since I was the only Black person there, I thought it might calm him to see me so I tried to engage with him. His name was Michael and he was from Jamaica. He was confused, not obviously mentally ill but just resigned, unresponsive and flat out refusing to go into his house, and it's no wonder. He'd lost complete control in there. I tried to persuade him to come back to the secure unit with us, at least to get a meal and a good night's sleep. He thought about it:

'I'm not going to hospital. No. Which one? The local one? I know that one. No. Not going there.'

'No, this is the new place in the big new hospital. They can give you somewhere to sleep and get you some food.'

I sat with him as we filmed and I began to feel responsible for him, and the more I engaged with him, the more I wanted him to get some help. After about an hour he finally decided to get in the ambulance and again, I found myself sitting with him. We spoke for about twenty minutes before it was decided that we should take him to the hospital, even though he didn't look as though he was experiencing any sort of breakdown. We thought at least he might get a good night's sleep and some food. Eventually, we all made our way to the hospital with the ambulance following our vehicle but ten minutes from our destination the ambulance began flashing its lights and slowing down. Our passenger was getting upset. Again, I had to climb inside and calm him, which I eventually did and we finally got to the hospital, but upon arrival he wouldn't get out of the ambulance. He was gripped with fear and very anxious so I climbed aboard again to see if I could talk to him. I felt I should do. He was alone and very vulnerable ... Plus, he looked just like my father. I sat and chatted with him, asked him if he wanted some toast or something.

'Toast. Yes.'

It was getting late now, we'd been with this man for about four hours and I could see our rather large security detail getting impatient, so I again put it to him that he should just get a good night's sleep in the unit and rest. He demolished the toast when it arrived, shoving huge chunks of it in his mouth till it was all gone, vanished in an instant, so I said:

'Let's go get some more. Come on, Michael, let's go get some more toast.'

'Toast. Okay. Okay.'

Finally, we climbed out of the back of the ambulance. But the fear again gripped him and he hesitated as we got inside the lobby, the reality of being in a hospital really beginning to sink in. By now I was quite uncomfortable with the fact that we were still filming. I could see Michael was getting more and more distressed and I felt as though what I was doing had crossed a line. I was making a documentary but I had got personally involved with this man and I didn't feel he needed a film crew with him as he went through the experience, so I stepped away. Just as I did so security upped the intensity and he was ushered away into the hospital, gently but firmly escorted by staff. It was tough to watch that fear sink in, the realisation that the ride was over and that he was on his way to a psychiatric ward. I didn't even know for sure that he was actually having a breakdown. He was just a man overwhelmed with his circumstances, alone and confused, and now he was heading for a hospital, heading into the system and, just like I had been, he was terrified. It's a particularly frightening moment in the process. I'm sure my father would have been indignant.

I'm happy to be a part of the growing conversation around race and mental health because too many people are falling victim to stigma when talking about our vulnerabilities could do much to help. Psychosis doesn't just happen to someone. There is a combination of different factors that can play a role in the onset of the illness. The more stress a person is under, the higher the chances are that someone could be vulnerable to psychosis. People should be made aware of the many contributing factors that could increase their vulnerability.

Genetics can predispose us to some kinds of mental health problems. The fact that my father had experienced mental health issues should really have put me on notice. Mental health conditions can pass on through generations and it wouldn't be unusual for a condition to skip a couple of generations. Adverse childhood experiences (ACEs) also contribute to the likelihood of suffering with mental ill health. It isn't like I had the most traumatic of childhoods, but growing up in a racist environment wasn't exactly stress-free. ACEs include events and traumas experienced in childhood like parental separation, parental incarceration, bullying, abuse and even poverty. All of these circumstances can increase a person's vulnerability, as does growing up in a city, with less social cohesion and more pollution, threats and noise.

In my case, there were other *precipitating* factors in my life at the time: dealing with the reality of the significance of my colour and how it would shape my career, and understanding how the white space moulded people's imaginations so that they couldn't see anything *other* than my colour. There were also *perpetuating* factors: the things I persisted in doing whilst I was ill. Continuing to smoke weed and regularly staying up late overstimulated my mind, which perhaps increased the severity of my condition. I'm as liberal as it comes where marijuana is concerned but even I've been surprised by the amount of times there has been a correlation between the drug and a person's psychosis. The young mind is very fragile and there are lots of physiological and neurochemical changes going on in inside the brain. The THC in the marijuana is toxic during this time and encourages overstimulation and increased mental activity.

Psychosis is now seen as a biopsychosocial illness, which means it is a condition concerning the interconnection between biology, psychology and socio-environmental factors. We take into account all of these different factors as they each can play a role in the development of the condition.

The final sequence of the film was me and my mother talking about my recovery. Again, filming gave us the space to talk about something we hadn't spoken about for years. Only now did I realise just what she had done for me: how she had nursed me back to health, kept a sharp eye on me as I was recovering and eventually put me back on the road. We drove to her old flat, the one I recovered in, and shot a sequence standing outside.

'This is where you came to recover, remember? This is where the old David came back,' she said.

'I don't think it was the old David, Mum, I think it was a new one.'

And the film ends.

*

Within the space of a week, I was back in Vancouver, about to start filming season four of *Supergirl*. I spent the first couple of months in a state of bewilderment, trying to process everything that had happened back in England, and going over everything that I'd learned. Wendie would check in from time to time, updating me on the edit. I trusted her, so was content to let her get on with putting it all together. I put the envelope containing my medical records on the bookshelf, fat with my secrets and ready to tell a tale. I almost forgot about it, shoving all my vulnerabilities down, almost hoping I could forget about them all over again. But I still wasn't out of the woods.

Eventually Wendie and my producer, Emma Hindley, were ready to show me the documentary in its rough but complete form. They carefully prepared me for the viewing by making sure I had support systems on hand in case anything triggered a reaction. I was fine because time had elapsed and I was in a different place emotionally. I felt secure enough to watch it with them and we all pressed play at the same time. They needn't have been worried. I absolutely loved it! I thought it was extremely well put together. The editing captured the fractured, visual quality of my experience. I was happy with the story it told. But it wouldn't be going out in the pre-arranged slot. In the end the BBC decided to place the film amongst two other films in a season of programmes dedicated to mental health, which meant that it would be a whole year before it would be seen. I was fine with that decision. I knew it was going to be shown at some point and I just carried on with my role in Vancouver.

Another long season of *Supergirl* passed and once again I returned to London, knowing the programme was going to be aired. I expected there to be press, but I wasn't really prepared to be talking about my trauma in such a vast public forum. Once or twice I found the interviews uncomfortable. Again, I was doing my professional best to publicise the show, but the subject matter was me and my pain and once or twice it got the better of me. I had to do an hour of radio plugs one day, short segments with stations across the country, cheery radio hosts in the mould of Alan Partridge, coming hot to me live from Radio Cheshire.

'Ed Sheeran and Justin Bieber there with "I don't care". Great song that. Kind of song to get you up in the morning and feeling good. Twenty minutes past the hour. In a minute we're going to be talking to the actor David Harewood who had a mental breakdown when he was twenty-three years old and now he's made a BBC documentary where he retraces his steps to find out what happened. But first we'll have the weather with Susan.'

Then I'd get the line producer in my ear telling me:

'Hi, David, thanks for doing this. Very interesting programme. Can you hear us okay?'

'Yep.'

'Very good. You're up after this next segment.'

'. . . light showers. Getting better tomorrow but you'll need your umbrella at the weekend, for sure.'

'Susan, thank you, always a pleasure. Now, we've got Hollywood actor and star of stage and screen David Harewood on the line to talk about his new documentary. David, tell us a little bit about it.'

Suddenly I'm live on air, wistfully talking about my mental breakdown in small, tight soundbites that explain the documentary, but it wasn't as if I was talking about a character I was playing, or a movie I was promoting. This was all deep, personal stuff. By the fourth round of interviews I was over it. I could have chewed my way out of the studio. I managed to complete all of them, but I just wanted to get the hell out of the building. A couple of days later I saw the first advert for the programme come up on the television and momentarily I panicked.

What the fuck have I done letting everyone into my pain?

I remember getting quite nervous about the whole thing, and when the night came that it was being broadcast, I decided not to watch it. I was suddenly extremely worried about how it would affect my name, my family and my career. I had to work hard to keep my shit together. Thankfully, I had a session with my therapist lined up, so we did an online session whilst it was on.

Everybody else in the house went to bed. Nobody watched it. Perhaps my anxiety had spread throughout the house. I wasn't sure but by the time the session was over, the house was quiet and dark. I just went to bed and lay there, wondering what would happen next.

I had nearly fallen asleep when my mobile phone started vibrating. Messages were flooding in so I sat up to turn it off, but just then the house phone began to ring. I jumped up as I didn't want to wake everybody up. It was my mother. She just wanted to say how much she'd enjoyed the programme and how well it had told the story. I was really chuffed. After the call I checked my phone and I had some amazingly supportive messages and emails, not just from friends but from professionals in the business too, all telling me what an impact the programme had made, not just publicly but on a personal level. I sat for a while in the dark, just thinking about what I'd done. It was out of my hands now, but the early signs were that it had hit the mark.

The next morning, I took the dog for a walk across the common, a daily ritual when I'm home. It gives me so much pleasure spending that early morning hour walking the dog, and I make the most of it when I can. We set off in our usual direction when a lady rushed over and thanked me for making the documentary. She said it would help a lot of people. I felt a little emotional, so I nodded and quickly moved on. Shortly thereafter another person approached to talk and this time we both started sobbing. I just about pulled myself out of that conversation when somebody else came over to speak to me. I began walking across the grass, avoiding people on the path. I just found it all a little too raw. I felt as if I'd shown everybody my most intimate, naked self. It was a pretty uncomfortable couple of days.

There were positive outcomes, too. Overnight, I'd become accessible to people. I was no longer an unapproachable TV actor, I was somebody with whom they could relate. After a while I began to settle down, and I wasn't bursting into tears every time someone mentioned the programme. We had some other smaller screenings and I did a few Q&As afterwards. I couldn't watch the show any longer, and left the room before it came on. For me, it's like watching another person, the man I used to be, and I can't help thinking he looks a little lost.

Soon after broadcast, I returned to work abroad. It was good to get away, to be honest. It had been a bruising trip. I needed to repair and to be away from England and its intensity. I was still processing everything and needed space to think it through. There is no better place to escape and just be yourself than Vancouver. It was lovely to be back. A number of people emailed and asked me to write a book having watched the documentary, but I never responded. Me? Write a book? Yeah, like that was ever going to happen. My brain was still scrambled by what I'd put myself through and I was waiting for everything to settle. I needed time.

A couple of months passed and I got an email from a publisher asking me to create an audiobook and, for some reason, it piqued my interest. We communicated on the phone for a couple of months and eventually I sent him something I'd written.

'This isn't an audiobook, David,' he said over a call. 'This is a full-on book. You should think about writing one.'

Pretty soon I met my literary agent, Natalie, and things seemed like they were coming together. Then news from China and the World Health Organization broke of a deadly virus that was spreading across the world, killing hundreds of people, and life just turned upside down. Filming was cancelled, the world was shutting down and within a week I was walking through a deserted Heathrow airport heading home to be with my family.

I know many, many people had a tough time during the first lockdown but my experience was different. This was the longest time I had spent with my family in nearly ten years. It was a welcome, long-earned rest. I'd finally stopped filling my time with projects and loved every minute. The lockdown gave me a chance to remember the things I care about. It gave me the chance to reassess all that I'd achieved in my life, everything I'd worked so hard to create.

One morning, I got up and just started writing. I wrote the chapter entitled 'The Ward' first, very quickly, and then followed that up with memories of my youth. It wasn't until I finally returned to Vancouver, when we'd resumed filming, that the true hard work began. I remember landing back in Canada, sailing through the empty airport and heading home in the car, straight into two weeks of isolation. What else to do but write, right? I picked up the big, brown envelope from the bookshelf containing my medical records and opened it. I'd been sitting with its unopened secrets for six months. Facing up to the truth of my psychotic breakdown was painful but it has given me a lot of freedom.

Up until writing this book, I had buried all the trauma under thirty years of graft and trying to survive as an actor. I had buried it so deep that I only had fleeting memories of some bizarre experiences I went through. Writing this memoir has meant taking a hard look at my deepest, darkest moment, understanding my vulnerabilities and being honest about them. I have had to muster courage and not be afraid to stand in my truth.

I may have firmer foundations than before I had my psychotic breakdown, but the subject of my race continues to be a huge issue in my life as the world around me changes. George Floyd's death created a lightning rod around the world in terms of addressing race and the treatment of Black people. Having a perspective in two different countries, I find the debate on race far more advanced in America than in the UK. Navigating that difference has sometimes landed me in difficulty.

Race and slavery represent an open wound in American society that bleeds to this day and I marvel when the scars and injustices of the past, such as the recent uncovering of mass graves in Tulsa and story of the white mob that massacred hundreds of innocent Black residents of the town of Greenwood, are openly acknowledged and memorialised. Pain and injustice acknowledged. In England, it would seem such acknowledgement isn't necessary because it's not supported by the data. Keep calm and carry on. And yet it is race that continues to shake the foundations of England's institutions as its imperialist history comes under new scrutiny. You'll send police to guard your statues from me should I have the temerity to climb upon them and look to tear them down, the apparatus of the state employed to check my passionate expression. And when the stately homes of England's green and pleasant land choose to tell you the truth about what you're appreciating, how it was paid for, you'll complain and say it's unnecessary. You do not want to hear this truth and will throw furious denials back in my face, the 'whataboutisms' hurling past me like West Indian fast balls whistling past my ears. You will not hear this. It appears to drive you mad. It seems to me that though 'race' sent me crazy thirty-odd years ago, it's sending many of you crazy now, as you wrestle with this new understanding that maybe, Black lives have mattered for centuries. It's just that you had no idea.

Until recently in the UK any talk about the issue of race and racism elicited angry denials and distraction. The UK government's recent Sewell report drives that point home. People challenging the existence of a problem at all were seen as gaslighting. I'm familiar with people telling me they can't even see what I know to be true. Blanket denial is one of the main reasons why Black people find it difficult living in the UK, which has a system from which they have to protect themselves and one in which they are confronted with daily micro-aggressions and experience a sense of powerlessness.

Travelling has helped me see the limitations of life in the UK. Years ago, I was a UK ambassador to Africa with the charity CAFOD, visiting an area of Kenya that had become so affected by climate change that people who had lived there for centuries could no longer continue to do so. It was so hot and dry that the cattle were dying from starvation. Hardly any food would grow. The charity was running programmes teaching farmers how to grow different, more durable crops as well as digging wells for irrigation. I arrived in one particular village after about a five-hour drive. When the villagers saw me and understood that I was representing both the charity and England, they decided to call the whole village out. The women sat on one side and the men on the other with the elders together at the front, watching me intently. One of them got up and made a speech in Swahili, referring to me as he did so. The crowd nodded, and gave appreciative smiles. After he'd finished I asked our guide what he had said and he told me that the elder had told everybody:

'One of our sons has returned as the *mzungu*, the big boss, foreigner, the white man. And he has brought with him assistance and knowledge. We must welcome our long-lost son. And thank him for the gifts that he brings.'

They were so used to seeing white representatives from England as the benefactors that seeing a Black Englishman in that position had called for a village meeting! Although a foreigner, *mzungu*, and an Englishman, to them I was still a long-lost son, to be welcomed and shown respect.

Since that fateful day when the man on the street told me to get the fuck out of his country, I have felt homeless in a sense. I have the feeling that I don't quite belong to the ground beneath my feet and it still makes me feel unsettled. After writing this book, I understand things better.

If you've experienced anything like what I have described in this book, I hope this gives you the strength to keep pushing for your dreams. You may have taken a back road, like me, through psychosis or mental ill health, but having been there and come through it, I hope you can apply what you've learned in a way that truly frees you to be the person you're meant to be. Psychosis will most likely change you, but it doesn't have to be the end of you. I'm thankful I came through it and I'm aware of how it helped me overcome my inhibitions and fear of failure.

Maybe if I'd come to this state of awareness years ago, my life would have been different, but I'm happy to have finally arrived at this place of peace and understanding of myself. I took time to sit with my demons and acknowledge the different parts of my identity that make up who I am. I will always be *mzungu*, foreigner, even 'white man' to some of my more 'authentically' Black brothers, but that's in their world. I just have to make sure I don't make it a truth in my own.

This long American swing I've been on for the last ten years is coming to an end now and the closing episodes of *Supergirl* are in their final edit. After six long years of filming, I'll be returning home to a different country from the one I left years ago, one that is now cut adrift from our European neighbours and sitting comfortably to the right of the room. The country's seemingly rising tide of populist nationalism reminds me of a time I've lived through before, only this time instead of people chasing me through gardens, they are writing newspaper columns and spewing division from social media, from radio shows and from parliamentary pews. This time there are no baseball bats, no cudgels. This time it's my mind that has to be nimble and quick to survive. And, after this long and difficult journey, it's stronger than ever. Of that, you can be sure.

Epilogue

The Subtle Misconception

What do you see when you look at me? Do you see a 'large Black man'? Do I threaten you, frighten you, make you feel uneasy? I often wonder why, because we've known each other for so long. I would have thought you knew me by now and yet it would appear that still, even after all these years, you do not really see me. Of course, we first met in the 1600s when you transported me from the shores of Africa to the small Caribbean island of Barbados, where you put me to work in the fields. Through my hard labour the island became one of the most profitable places in the world. Money flowed into your pockets and you used it to build many of your finest buildings. And although my portrait doesn't hang in any of these fine mansions, it was my sweat and hard labour that enabled you to build them. I worked hard in those fields, cutting sugar cane from first light of the morning to the setting of the sun and with intense heat burning down upon me.

I really wasn't expected to last long but last I did, better than those you tried before me. I had strength, unlike those 'red legs' you brought over from home. I could stand the heat. And to control me, you came up with a very different set of laws from the ones that governed the cobbled streets of England. The Slave Codes you wrote gave you control of me, allowed you to punish, beat, burn, rape or kill me with almost complete impunity. Beat and kill me you did. You were lord and master for real. And when, eventually, you had to bow to public pressure and give me liberty, did you give me a single penny of the money given to you by the British government for the loss of me? Well, I guess you did give me something, you gave me your name: 'Harewood'.

Richard Harewood was the first. Born a slave on the Thickets Plantation, he met and married Betty Rose who had a son called Benjamin Harewood in 1840, who grew strong and met and married Mary Elvira Cain. They had a son, Nathaniel Harewood, in 1867 who also grew strong and married Georgina Coulthurst Newton. They had a son, Herbert Christopher Harewood, in 1900, who again grew strong and married Druscilla Viola Walcott. In 1937 they had a son, Romeo Cornelius Harewood, who grew up and came to England, where he met and married my wonderful mother, Mayleen, and together they had a son, me.

I am another Harewood, from a line of Harewoods, finding my place in a very different world from those once created by you, but even so, after all these years you do not really see me. If I stand very still, and know my place, don't make too much noise or draw too much attention to myself, it's possible to walk around your house, from room to room, without you noticing. I watch you. I see you play and I watch you love. You barely notice I'm there, even though I've lived here all my life.

But, not too long ago, when we were all locked down in our homes shielding from the deadly virus, we watched as a 'large Black man' like me in Minneapolis was killed in front of our very eyes under the knee of an American policeman. We had seen this sort of thing before: on the news when a 'large Black man' was out running and shot dead; when another was found asleep in his car shot dead; when yet another was shot dead selling cigarettes. But it was the death of this 'large Black man', George Floyd, that sent a wave of revulsion around the world, and brought millions of people out onto the street.

I was with you when we heard them outside, a mass of faces, white, Black, brown, Asian, a pulsating throng of youthful protest, walking up the street. I had to go. I joined the crowd and walked alongside them as a thousand voices acknowledged my existence and proclaimed in the street that 'Black Lives Matter'! It was thrilling. And when I saw the statue that you'd built to celebrate one of my overlords finally topple, I felt a strange emotional stirring in the pit of my stomach. And yes, your heroes got daubed with paint, and the authorities jostled and held the line. You wrote about it and took pictures of Black warriors carrying wounded soldiers from the field. It was a heady time. When I came home that afternoon, as usual I kicked off my shoes and headed to the kitchen, ready to feast on the food you'd cooked to nourish your loved ones, and as I open the fridge you turned to me and said:

'I SEE YOU.'

I was stunned. Caught short briefly. You saw me? We spoke. I must admit, I didn't find it easy. Talking about my struggle brings up bad feelings. It's traumatic for me to go there, you see, and most of the time you don't believe me anyway so it can be difficult. I tried to speak but I found myself struggling to keep it together. Many of you even ordered multiple books off the internet in an effort to understand how on earth you could have missed the fact that I'd been here all along and fighting so hard to be heard.

After I'd settled down we sat at the kitchen table and I told you about the day I saw a brown princess cheered by the British people, how it made me feel. Strangely emotional watching, engaged as never before. More 'pomp and soul' than 'pomp and ceremony'. I had such hopes that day.

But others came to your house and they did not see me and spoke disparagingly about both me and the princess, and I watched to see if you had the courage to introduce us. Have you the courage to stand up for me? When there is booing as my allies take the knee and outrage when a supermarket features me in a Christmas advert? Will you see the obsession as they chase away the brown princess and attempt to poison my mind against her? It's almost working, I'm sick of hearing about it all myself, now, my God she must be strong. Relentless negativity, cries of 'battles' and 'war', yet upstairs, likely in the very same household where that revered family resides, random hand towels from Jeffrey Epstein's private island probably sit neatly folded, fluffed and ready for use, and nobody says a word. They will not tolerate me. It's okay. I see them too. And I have enough patience for you all to finish reading the books you ordered off the internet to help you understand.

My colour is the most obvious thing about me but who is the man inside? Do you see me? Can you imagine me a King of England or the last Son of Mars? A roguish lover, a prime minister or the deputy head of the CIA? What do you see me as, when I walk down Gower Street on an early spring morning?

I guess that's the subtle misconception. I can see myself as any-thing. My imagination knows no limits. I am a Harewood, off to the Royal Academy of Dramatic Art, smiling as I make my way from the station, Euston normally, turning the corner and head-ing south. I'll soon be at the bookshop, the crossroads that will take me to the Marlborough Arms, fun to be had in there, and on to Tottenham Court Road. University College London to my left, where the beer flows a pound a pint and I dance a drunken jig to New Order's 'Blue Monday'. Just a little further, past the hotels and there, on your left, is my destination, the stepping stone to the rest of my life and everything I am today.

Although I don't know it yet, this 'subtle misconception' will be my undoing when I'm told that I cannot play this or I cannot play that simply because of the colour of my skin. It won't be long before such thinking has me confused to the point of madness as I try to wrap my head around a whole new reality. But at this moment in time, I'm still young and idealistic, still thinking of the characters I'm destined to play, just like my heroes on *Parkinson*. For now, it's day one, and I'm about to walk into the building that will change my life forever, the Royal Academy of Dramatic Art.

Acknowledgements

There are many people who have come into my life over the years, many actors, friends and colleagues who have each given me support, friendship and guidance as the time has gone by: too many to name but if you've taken the time to read this book, let me take this opportunity to tell you how much I appreciate you all.

Professionally, a huge thank you to Nicki, Barry and Vikram, my reps, who all signed me up long before the bright lights came on. They've often shown more belief in me than I sometimes show in myself and I'm grateful to have each of them in my corner. To Natalie and Carole for guiding me through all this, and everyone at Bluebird for making it possible.

Personally, a big thank you to my family, who give me so much joy. I may have missed the better part of the last ten years with you, but how you've grown into the women you are makes an old man very proud.

There are some people I'd like to give a particular shout-out to. Without them, I'm not really sure I'd be here to tell this story. To Nick, Jeremy, Danny and Jane, old friends who took care of me when I was most in trouble, a massive and hearty thank you for everything you did for me when I was ill. I see now I buried all that you did along with the pain I went through, but I hope you now know just how much love I have for you all.

And finally, perhaps the biggest thank-you of all goes to Mr Eric Reader, the English teacher who first told me I should be an actor. His inspiring words that day set me on course that though at times has been difficult, I would not have changed for the world. Words made into action. A young boy's life set in motion. Thank you, Eric Reader. A+.

Illustration and Text Credits

Text credits

Plate section image credits

David Harewood was born in Birmingham, England. His parents are originally from Barbados and they moved to England in the 1950s and 1960s. He grew up in Small Heath. He trained as an actor at London's Royal Academy of Dramatic Art and is best known for his roles in *Homeland* and *Supergirl*. David's critically acclaimed BBC documentary *Psychosis and Me* received a BAFTA nomination for best documentary. He was awarded an MBE for his services to acting in 2012.

David is married, has two daughters and is an avid Birmingham City FC fan. *Maybe I Don't Belong Here* is his first book.